PANORAMA OF WORLD ART

———

ART OF THE BYZANTINE WORLD

ART OF THE

BYZANTINE WORLD

Text by CHRISTA SCHUG-WILLE

HARRY N. ABRAMS, INC. Publishers NEW YORK

Front end papers:

Joshua and the Angel. Part of the *Joshua Roll*. Height 12$^1/_2$", overall length 33'. First half of tenth century.
Ms. Gr. 431, Biblioteca Vaticana, Rome

Back end papers:

Sarcophagus of the Two Brothers. Tomb for two people. Marble, 44$^1/_2$ × 83$^7/_8$". Second third of fourth century.
From a cemetery at San Paolo Fuori le Mura. Lateran Museum, Rome

Translated from the German by E. M. Hatt

Standard Book Number: 8109-8020-7
Library of Congress Catalogue Card Number: 75-92912

Contents

Introduction

"Roman statecraft, Greek culture, and Christian belief are the three wellheads of Byzantine development. If any of these three had been missing, Byzantium as we know it could not have existed. It was only the synthesis of Hellenistic culture and the Christian religion with Roman governmental forms which could have caused that historical phenomenon, known as the Byzantine state, to arise" (G. Ostrogorsky).

These constituents of Byzantium as a power are also recognizable in the history of what was to become more or less an official and imperial art. But if there had been nothing beyond these three, then obviously "Byzantine art" might equally have been born in Rome, a city where the imperial system had been evolved, which was steeped in Hellenistic culture, and where the presence of Saint Peter's tomb supplied the earliest of all justifications for establishing the Christian Church. Clearly the synthesis, in the form it finally assumed, could only have been achieved in specific conditions and required outside elements which did not exist in Rome at that time.

When we speak today of Byzantine art, we are not setting it within strictly geographical limits but referring to the art of a world within a world, the expansion and contraction of which was continually conditioned by the vicissitudes of politics. From its earliest years, this art was based on one capital city, the seat of an Emperor who was simultaneously sovereign prince and high priest. It is an art which enriched that of the Western world yet remained largely independent of reciprocal influences from it. In this characteristic self-sufficiency, which showed itself in a quite individual attitude to the classical inheritance, lies our justification for treating Byzantine art as a phenomenon apart and not as a chapter in the continuous history of Western art, nor even as a parallel development touching it at certain points and moving along at the same pace. In spheres other than that of art, there was of course an inevitable linking, since the technical and other discoveries of an epoch end up by being shared, and historical events affect communities other than those immediately implicated.

When Constantine founded his capital of Constantinople on the site of the ancient Byzantium, the art of the Western world was in a period of decline. When Justinian was building up his empire of the East, that of the West was disintegrating as a result of the mass migrations which were weakening its structure. By the time of the Renaissance, the fifteenth-century cultural revival which brought classical art to life again, the last remnants of the Byzantine Empire were falling into the hands of the conquering Turks. Between the collapse of the old Roman Empire and the fall of Constantinople in 1453, the Byzantine Empire flourished as a highly organized state; for many of those centuries it was the only one in the whole of the then known world.

Starting with this advantage, and favored by its geographical location, its political and cultural strivings soon took on a peculiar importance. The Mediterranean basin was the center of Western classical art and political power, and in the middle of it lay Rome, which in the outgoing classical period had seized the leadership of that world before Constantinople was founded. It was not only the foundation of Constantinople which marked the division of the western Mediterranean world from the eastern but also the division of the Roman Empire into separate halves which henceforth became independent. The consequent regrouping and redistribution of powers and privileges brought about a situation in which the claims of the East could no longer be brushed aside. When Theodosius I died in 395, he left the two parts of his empire to his two sons. Arcadius ruled in the East, Honorius in the West, and the Western capital lost much of its luster since it was no longer the sole seat of government—Trier and Milan both disputed its preeminence. But as long as a city such as Antioch could challenge Constantinople as the political capital, claiming almost equal standing, the East was not much more than an offshoot of the old Roman Empire. Under Theodosius II (408–50) Constantinople's claim to supremacy was asserted firmly and this was made apparent in the building of her great landward walls.

The conclusive event which was to put the state of Byzantium on a solid foundation was still in the future. Constantine had indeed routed Maxentius at the Battle of the Milvian Bridge in 312, and proclaimed, in Rome, that henceforward Christianity was the state religion, but it was only under Justinian (527–65), who counts as the real founder of the Byzantine state, that the ideals of statehood and Christianity were put on an equal plane.

In the years of Justinian's reign one fruitful achievement succeeded another, each leaving a lasting imprint on the new state and its new arts. Justinian was an Illyrian and his wife Theodora came from Syria, so that the mere fact of their accession imparted, as it were, an oriental bias. Justinian's efforts to restore the Roman Empire were not meant to give back to the West its old importance; they were meant to capture it and place it under firm obedience to Byzantium. The final result was not the rehabilitation but the destruction of the Roman Empire as such.

Justinian's attitude to the art of Antiquity also had its ambiguous aspects. Of course there was no sudden eclipse of existing graphic and sculptural styles; as forms of expression, they were irreplaceable, but regardless of this, the pagan elements in them were inexorably purged away. Pagan and heretical teachers were expelled from the public university at Constantinople, and the long pre-Christian tradition of the Athenian schools of philosophy was abruptly broken by the closing down of the academies. In the Byzantine Empire itself all manifestations of the heathen past were extirpated once and for all. The administration of the state and the establishment of new canons of art were equally the concern of the Emperor in Byzantium.

For his rule and conduct of affairs, Justinian took over the Roman legal code and gave it a new written form which placed all the central powers—governmental, legislative, and administrative—in his own hands. It is significant that after the Nika insurrection of 532 the additions to, and the commentary on, his Code were all translated into Greek. The Nika insurrection was important, and dangerous too, for it brought into unwelcome prominence vexed questions of precedence: questions, for instance, as to whether the Emperor's claims overrode certain claims implicit in Church dogma. The revolt had its uses—later it could be cited as an excuse for "preventive measures." False doctrine and rebellious opinion directed against Church or State could lead to a similar revolt: so both sought to protect and arm themselves at all points by clarifying and defining dogma as well as law. That was possible only with the concentration of all powers under one authority. The Nika insurrection also dealt a serious blow to the Empire. The heart of the capital was smashed to pieces, the great basilicas of Constantine and his heirs were razed to the ground, the first splendid Hagia Sophia was reduced to rubble. Justinian took advantage of this destruction to rebuild in a new style; Hagia Sophia was no longer to be a five-aisled church of the Roman type but a prototype that was to be followed for many years: the domed basilica developed from an octagonal ground plan, the scheme chosen by Justinian in 527 for the first of his churches. The square with an octagon superimposed on it was quite a usual plan in the east, particularly in Syria where it had evolved during the fifth and early sixth centuries, and it had become standard by the time of Justinian who summoned Syrian architects to his court. Here, within a very short time, the domed church, decisive for the future of Byzantine architecture, was perfected. This abandonment of the Western, Roman tradition of building in favor of innovations from Eastern lands is a milestone in the history of art; it must also have colored Justinian's ideas on the form which the state was to take and as to where he should look for his models. That this type of building must have had some affinity with his political concepts may well be proved by his church in Ravenna which he had erected as a counterpart to Saints Sergius and Bacchus in Constantinople; it was likewise his palace church, and well placed to assert the imperial claims of the East in this place, while at the same time heartening the Orthodox in their polemical strife with the Arians.

In the seventh century Germanus, the Patriarch, described the Church in general as "the Heaven on earth in which God from on High walks forth." So too, under Justinian, the ruler had to have his place in this Heaven on earth and this explains why the Emperor and Empress are shown with haloes taking their positions above in Heaven in the San Vitale mosaics at Ravenna. This is something that was as alien to classical Roman art as to the Early Christian art of the West, and brought in an entirely new element. It is perhaps best grasped if it is understood under the category of "abstract representation." This trend showed itself in other ways: the introduction of the *iconostasis* (screen adorned with icons), behind which the sacrifice of the mass was performed; and the new church music including hymns which reduced the multiplicity of harmonic forms to unison singing. Then there was the greater intimacy of the domed church in which all who shared in the celebration were grouped together in company under the dome. A comparison of the two imperial mosaics at San Vitale (see pages 96 f.) with the Old Testament mosaics in the same church, which are more in the tradition of Constantine and not far removed from late classical Antiquity, shows what was lost here and what was gained.

With such characteristics as these, the art of Justinian's time stands at a crossroads and is not easily assessed. On the one hand, it concludes the art of Antiquity and fulfills the tendencies which had been evolving for two hundred years; on the other, it is a starting point for the epoch later known within the framework of European history as the Middle Ages. But while the outlook of the Middle Ages in the West was definitely restricted to Europe, even when the aspirations of the Roman Empire were being revived, Justinian was able to free himself from the limited horizons of a solely Mediterranean policy. He reconquered Italy, Africa, and part of Spain while aspiring to restore the whole Roman inheritance. He was forced to wage his Italian campaigns in order to regain the vitally important Mediterranean basin, but once this was achieved he sought no more adversaries in the barbarian West. He now strove after world dominion, and his chief rivals were the Sassanian Persians with whom he had had to share world trade from China and India to the Germanic North. The trade with China, India, and Turkestan, which the Sassanians were determined to monopolize, was vital to the Byzantine economy. Trade with the East meant heavy capital commitment and the individual merchant was so much subject to recurrent risks that the loss of even one ship was enough to ruin him. So, in making it possible at all—through state guarantees on a large scale—Justinian succeeded in bringing all trade under state control. Profit margins, which depended upon the trade routes through Persia, therefore affected the state more than a little. Thus the blocking of the trade route through Persia by the Sassanians—and the attack by them on a friendly trading partner—gave enough cause for the unleashing of the Persian Wars. More through the precedents it set than through the increased burdens it threw on the state, it led to a further increase in the state's claims to overriding authority in all spheres. The preoccupations of scholars, the organization of religion, the conduct of trade, the promulgation and administration of the law, all were now under state control and this authority no longer had any rival in the western part of the Empire. Under Justinian, the western and eastern sections were fast drifting apart. The Eastern Empire was setting its house in order through a new organization of the Church, a new political system, and above all through new social structures.

There have been attempts to simplify this process and to concentrate on two chief aspects of it: on the commanding position achieved by the monastic orders of the Eastern Church under Justinian, and on the decisive role of the army in the state. The clericalization, proceeding from the monasteries, of all intellectual concepts, and the falling of all administration more and more into the hands of the army, tended directly toward the concentration of power in the state which had, however, to separate this trend from its initiators, for no state could afford so great a degree of dependence. In their attitudes to art and culture generally the Eastern monks were not, as the Western ones were, in the Greco-Roman tradition, for their roots were in Asia Minor. This explains the totally different approach to figurative art, the visible turning away from classical precepts, and (even more significantly) severance from every Western and Roman art form nourished by sources so alien to their way of thinking. This transformation of the basic outlook, the new conception of the form of the state, the reordering of the social structure, the shaping of state policies with an eye to world politics, and the new leaders of the state's established religion and of culture—these were all forces which shaped the direction of the future and the elements of the old Roman state passed on in the new, i.e., Greek culture and the Christian religion.

Disorders which broke out after Justinian's death carried these trends forward to an even more decisive stage. Slav invasions of the Balkan territories opened the way to new influences as well as, in the long run, to Byzantine influence in more northerly Russia. The Persian Wars, the strengthened military position resulting from them, and the settling of mercenaries from the east, further changed the social pattern. Common interests (including the need to rout common enemies) had meant the peaceful coexistence of the Church and the military, but a clash was bound to come when their interests no longer coincided. It came in the form of the iconoclastic conflict which arose out of relations toward the Arabs, newly emerged in succession to the Persians as challengers to the Byzantines for a position of world dominance, a conflict which resulted in the triumph of the Orthodox faith and in the wider dissemination of that form of Byzantine art rightly known as "Byzantine classical." The role of iconoclasm was of course a crucial one in shaping the history of art. It was during the reign of Leo III (717–41) that the struggle burst into the open. This ruler was known as "the Isaurian" though he came from North Syria rather than Isauria in Asia Minor. He had been Strategos (General) of the Themes of Anatolia (a *theme* was a grouping of imperial provinces, and these were later divided according to their military structures) and after a revolt against the weak Theodosius III had been called to the throne. He was also known as *Sarakenophron* ("Friend of the Saracens") because he had sought Arab support at the time of this revolt. The Arabs were fundamentally opposed to the representation of living beings and had already instigated one outbreak of iconoclasm; the Christians who most set themselves against "images and idols" happened to be those who were nearest the soldiers—and the fight against the Arabs—in Asia Minor. They were especially hostile to the monks and mistrustful of the growing power of the Church. In Byzantine art, works representing divine beings were not solely for edification, but were objects of veneration and thus instruments of power. Leo III accordingly ordered the destruction of all such works. As he wished also to make his proscription prevail throughout the West, he was soon in conflict with Rome and Pope Gregory III (734–41). The Byzantine military units in Italy took exception to this ban and united themselves with the Lombards. The schism between Byzantium and the West was only deepened by Byzantine iconoclasm, by Byzantium's relations with the pagan East, and by the fact that many of her generals were of Syrian origin. A further aggravation was the organization of the state, resting on the twin pillars of monasticism and militarism. Even the end of the iconoclastic troubles and the restoration to its former place of the controversial type of art was not able to close the gap. The West made its standpoint clear at the Synods of Frankfurt (794) and Paris (825) and proved to be as much against the destruction of works of art as against the worship of them; the purpose of these works, it was asserted, was to enlighten and to teach sacred history. The taking up of this position by the West in the quarrel with Byzantium led in the end to the crowning of Charlemagne (800) in Saint Peter's, Rome, but it is to be noted that the coronation ceremonial followed the models of Byzantium closely. The attempt at reconciliation which was made by Charlemagne when he proposed marriage to the Empress Irene was thwarted by the court of Byzantium in the crowning of Nicephorus the Logothete as Emperor in 802.

After Byzantium had freed herself from the West and the iconoclast troubles had died away, it was possible for a Greco-Byzantine state to emerge, evolving its own nationhood, one "true-believing" Church, and a flourishing civil power—which, on account of its political and military successes, could afford to support the Patriarch of Constantinople in his assertion of absolute autonomy against the spiritual claims of Rome. The old enemies in the East were repulsed, the whole of the Balkans was reconquered, the Empire was as great as it had been in the time of Justinian, and internal order prevailed.

The Church began its missionary work in the Balkans and created for itself there a new and decisive sphere of influence, into which Russia was soon drawn. The new states not only absorbed the new religion but also the culture and form of government of the country which sent out the missionaries; their art from that time onward was "Byzantine" in most senses of the word.

The Macedonian Emperors contributed power to one new element in the flourishing state which they inherited: the nobility. These were cultured and talented families forming an upper class of citizen (and perhaps, under the Comneni, a military caste). Under the Macedonians there was a new kind of national cultural awareness, a rebirth of the Greek tradition, the "Macedonian Renaissance" which lasted from 829 until 976. Those who carried the movement forward lived primarily in the capital. Their tastes were so remarkably enlightened and so clearly in favor of the preeminence of classical art and philosophy over theology that there could not fail to be protest from the conservative large-scale property owners and provincial military groups, who emphasized the priority of the Turkish menace. But it really seems to have been the activities of the Comnenus dynasty, which had in fact emerged from the military elite, that sped the Empire to its decline. The Norman Crusaders whose help had been enlisted showed themselves as more dangerous than the danger they were supposed to be averting, and in the end Byzantium had to fight simultaneously against them and the Turks. The wars indeed contained victories for the Byzantines, but the remilitarization of the state disturbed economic life and led to a heavy load of taxation. A policy stemming from alliances based solely on military considerations, and the eternal campaigning and consequent expense, sapped its strength and finally undermined imperial authority. Occasional victories in the field could not blind people to deterioration elsewhere, and the exaggerated love of power of the last of the Comneni, the Emperor Andronicus Comnenus, brought about complete collapse. As the Normans, fresh from the conquest of Salonika, were advancing on Constantinople in 1185, the enraged mob turned on Andronicus and tore him limb from limb in the street. In 1204, Constantinople fell into the hands of the Crusaders. Events after this can only be described as a decline and fall.

The blossoming and withering of the Byzantine Empire went hand in hand, throughout these years, with the spread of Orthodox belief and Byzantine art. Western Europe, with only the occasional sign of resistance, accepted the latter into its own official art and replied with some direct flashes of influence of its own.

Venice and Sicily had close connections with Byzantium, both friendly and hostile. Venice's dependence had meant friendship in the eleventh century but had resulted in the assertion by force of a monopoly position in trade in the twelfth century. At this time came the internal adornment of Saint Mark's, rendered as a service to Venice by the once powerful overlord, Byzantium. Venice sent to Constantinople for the best artists and craftsmen. The other aspirant to Byzantium's glory, Norman Sicily, attempted with the help of mosaic artists from the capital to take on a little of the splendor of the old imperial court. It had no national art tradition on which to build, which the Byzantine workers could have adapted or diluted, but Venice of the thirteenth century certainly had and knew how to exploit Byzantine skills and how to graft the imported art forms into their own Italian styles which in the thirteenth and fourteenth centuries were stamped unmistakably with them.

At that time Macedonia was the most important European mainland province of the Byzantine Empire. Justinian's northern limit had been the Danube. While the iconoclast struggle was raging, the Slav immigrants and the Bulgars had been a real threat to the Empire, but through their submission and their acceptance of the Orthodox form of Christianity they actually served to prolong the life of Byzantine culture, so that it outlived the state which gave it birth. Here again, the close alliance between this culture and Christianity was a decisive element in its long survival. Moreover, that state apparatus which had been so closely bound up with Christianity, and was so much an inheritance from the old Roman Empire, took hold abroad and lasted. The Bulgar khans and the Russian grand dukes even added the title of "Caesar" to that of "Basileus" in some cases; "Caesar" endured for a long time in the form of "Czar" or "Tsar." So it is not to be wondered that at the beginning of the venture, the sending of missions to the Slavs was not unconnected with political aspirations. Charlemagne had pushed his Pannonian frontier as far as the Danube, but the alliance of the enlarged Moravian empire with the powers of Western Christendom would have meant subordination for the Slavs who saw their best hope to lie in union with the still pagan Bulgars and with Byzantium. When the Moravians appointed Byzantine missionaries the Bulgar khan was in no position to resist them strenuously. Cyril and Methodius, brothers and missionaries, belonged to that group of monks trained in the propagation of the faith who were available to serve in such circumstances as these. In 864, when a year of missionary activity had elapsed, the Bulgar khan accepted baptism; and Khan Boris was clever enough to secure for the Church in Bulgaria its own patriarch, and to insist on the Slavonic language for services. There was a comparable situation in Russia, where Saint Vladimir, Grand Duke of Kiev, took over Christianity, state structure, and culture from Constantinople. Both of these rulers saw in Constantinople, at that time enjoying its greatest period, the only example to copy. It may even be said that, because of the threefold model just mentioned, Byzantium was always preferred to Rome. The imperial art of Byzantium was part of ceremonial and of court life, part even of the administration, and as such Kiev took it over. Since Justinian, architecture had not been solely the servant of religion, for civic requirements had also dictated the form and disposition of buildings, and Kiev not only imitated the styles but also the layout of the city center. Yaroslav the Wise (1019–54) copied whole areas of the city of Constantinople, even the triumphal way from the Golden Gate to the imperial palace bordered by the greatest churches. The Koimesis church was built after one of the same name which stood by the Blachernae Palace in Constantinople. This reflection of Byzantine state, religious, and court life was the rule in Russia until well into the nineteenth century, whatever changes other influences may have brought. The paintings—as devotional objects—which again abounded once the iconoclasts had lost their last battle, were eagerly copied. The icon, the painting worthy of veneration, is a Byzantine art form that was brought to perfection in Russia—indeed it became the principal interest of Russia's figurative artists.

Not only did Russia wholeheartedly accept and develop the icon tradition, but that other object of iconoclast wrath, the monastic orders, became part of the structure of Russian life and culture. There is no doubt that the monks played a vital role in the development of Russo-Byzantine culture and in its long endurance. Here there is a difference to be noted between East and West. Such a close connection, from the way it persisted, seems to have been an essential part of Byzantine culture. Byzantine monasticism both differs from and yet in a definite way echoes that of the West. The growth of the Carolingian state was dependent on the monks as bearers both of culture and of the burdens of court administration. Carolingian achievements in the cultural sphere also owed much to the monasteries. Western monks were stamped largely with

The Good Shepherd. Ceiling painting (after Wilpert) in the Chamber of the Good Shepherd. First half of third century. ▶
Coemeterium Maius, Rome

Augustinian attitudes; those of Mount Athos, who preserved their own tradition long after the fall of Byzantium, were altogether different in outlook rather than comparable.

Byzantine culture did in fact transmit to the Western world many of the elements of late Antiquity, in some cases giving new functions to old forms, and finding in the fusion of Eastern and Western characteristics an individual style. For certain regions of the West such elements had all the charm of novelty and proved fruitful in quite another way. After Constantinople had fallen to the Turks, it was the Russians who became masters in the East. Men versed in Greek thought and achievement came to Italy, to Florence and Venice, then centers of the Renaissance. They were received as transmitters of a new classical cultural inheritance already enjoyed and put to profitable use by Byzantium in her heyday. However, they did not bring with them the monastic attitude of mind to the interpretation of classical canons. What they had to offer was an urbane humanism, that of the Palaeologan renaissance, a humanism which came into its own very late in the life of the Empire and one which, in the years of decline, could be summed up only as a weary resignation to fate. It was a humanism strikingly exemplified by Theodorus Metochites when he said, "We are but inheritors." Byzantine culture had been a phenomenon apart; moreover, its character, as an extension of the imperial will and one expression of state requirements, had bound it too closely to the social structure of premedieval times. There was none of the freedom which the West managed to win for itself in this period of rejuvenation, as country after country equipped itself with new economic, social, political, and spiritual structures for a fuller life—a culture of unprecedented scope and quality.

ART OF THE EARLY CHRISTIAN CHURCH

The beginnings of Christian iconography are known to us only through sepulchral art. Tombs with fresco decoration dating from the end of the second century still survive. First-century Christians attached great importance to the separation of their burial places from those of the pagans since, as Tertullian said, there is nothing particularly objectionable about living with pagans, but to die with them, or indeed to lie in death with them, is quite inadmissible. In later times the Early Christian cemeteries were called catacombs, and thereafter forgotten and lost to sight until well into the sixteenth century. It is to twentieth-century archaeological investigation of Early Christian sites that we owe our knowledge of them.

Adam and Eve. Detail of ceiling painting in the Chamber of the Good Shepherd (cf. page 13)

The Christian religion differed from all current pagan creeds in its unswerving belief in Salvation in the world to come, in "the Resurrection to life eternal through Jesus Christ, Our Lord," as the burial service promised. This belief in salvation is the fundamental element in all Early Christian sepulchral art, indeed in all Early Christian art that has been transmitted to us. The theme of deliverance from all perils in the hereafter is implicit not only in the content but also in the form of the catacomb paintings. In these murals there is no hint of grief or mourning. Exuberantly leafy bowers, with tendrils and garlands in bright colors on a brilliant ground, adorn ceilings and walls. The composition of the ceiling decorations shows unmistakably the influence of secular paintings from the houses of wealthy Romans, such as the paintings which have come down to us from Nero's Domus Aurea, in Rome, and from the country houses of Roman gentlemen in Pompeii.

The central subject depicted on the ceiling (page 13) is a symbolic representation of the One from whom all salvation comes, and the parable form has been chosen. The Good Shepherd delivers from all harm the sheep of His flock, provided that they look to Him for deliverance. The Christian conveys this by raising his hands aloft and gazing upward to God. For this reason, even in the earliest third-century ceiling groups, a female figure in the *orant* (Latin *orare,* to pray) attitude is always present, imploring salvation, together with Old Testament scenes illustrating the theme of salvation arranged round the representation of the Saviour. There is, for example, Moses striking water from the rock to save the thirsting Israelites in the wilderness. An even clearer allusion to deliverance from the perils of death and to the resurrection after death is a painting of Jonah. Having spent three days and nights in the belly of the whale, he has now escaped from the monster's jaws and is resting in the gourd vine's shade. In contrast, another scene in the encircling group represents the Fall of the first man and woman in Eden (see facing page).

There are no New Testament scenes whatsoever in the third-century catacombs. This was due to some extent to a reluctance, rooted in Jewish tradition, to paint likenesses; most emphatically proscribed were representations of God. When Constantia, sister of the Emperor Constantine, asked Eusebius, a Father of the Church and Bishop of Caesarea, for a picture of Christ, he refused on the grounds that the making of such a picture was not permitted to Christians. This proscription was probably based on a strict interpretation of the Ten Commandments, forbidding the making of graven images. However, we have established the existence, as early as the opening years of the third century, of a figurative art among the Christians of Rome so highly developed that a longer tradition must be postulated.

Moses Strikes Water from the Rock. End of fourth century. Fresco in the Cripta della Peorelle. Catacomb of Callixtus, on the Appian Way, Rome

The Story of Susanna. Wall painting. End of third century. From the catacombs of the basilica of Saints Peter and Marcellinus, Rome

The *orant*, a female figure with hands raised in prayer, is the earliest and most persistent image in Early Christian art. Since she also appears on men's tombs we may conclude that she does not represent the dead person praying for redemption. Even in the second half of the second century she appears in catacomb pictorial groupings in close association with the Good Shepherd. When she is found alone it is often with the inscription PETE PRO NOBIS ("pray for us"). Therefore it seems a fair assumption that the *orant* represents the soul that has attained eternal life—but whether it is the soul of the one departed, or a generalization of the Christian soul which has achieved salvation through faith, is something which has to be decided separately each time she appears. In the illustration above, the *orant* is beyond all doubt a character with a role in the scene. Susanna between two Elders is beseeching God as a believer that she may be saved. In other depictions of Biblical events we see the male counterpart of this same concept: Daniel in the lions' den, shown as an *orant*. This scene signifies that the Christian should endure a martyr's death with courage, for God will deliver him from the grave.

The Dead Appearing Before Christ. Beginning of fifth century. Sepulcher in the Catacomb of Domitilla, Rome

Orpheus, according to ancient myth, brought joy and good fortune to the animals who followed him as he played his lyre. The shepherd bearing a calf on his shoulder was a subject that appealed to the artists of Antiquity. "Pastor" is the name given to ministers of the Christian Church, and Christ's command to Peter was, "Feed my lambs." Christ also pronounced the parable of the Good Shepherd whose life is at the service of his flock, and the Good Shepherd became the symbol for salvation through Christ. To the concept of Orpheus and the animals, taken over from legend, that of the Good Shepherd and the redemption of souls was closely linked, so that the wall painting above may be taken to allude to Christ.

Likewise the representation of Christ as the sun-god in his sun chariot was inspired by a pagan model. *Sol Invictus* is Helios himself, who ousted the sun-god of the Mithraic cult. Mithraism had many adherents among the soldiers of Rome and was among them a formidable rival to the Christian religion of salvation; for this cult too had its salvation theme in the form of a youthful hero who sacrificed a bull to the sun-god. This cult, born in Persia, had traveled with the Roman soldiers to provinces where Christianity had already made considerable headway and was inextricably associated with the Roman concept of the Sun-Emperor. In the catacomb mosaic, the pagan presentation of this theme was emphatically challenged—as though to say, "You worship Helios, but here you have the one true and invincible Sun-God—Christ as *Sol Invictus*." The Christian meaning of Redemption conveyed in the gold-ground mosaic found under Saint Peter's, Rome, is made clear by the various pictorial elements: for in the tendrils of the vines is another Redemption scene which only Christian art would make use of, a theme quite alien to the Mithraic cult—the deliverance of Jonah.

◀ *Christ-Orpheus.* Wall painting. Third century. Catacomb of Domitilla, Rome

Christ as Sun-God. Mosaic. c. 300. From the so-called Julian Tomb. Necropolis under Saint Peter's, Rome

Trough-shaped sarcophagus. Marble, 29¹/₂ x 94¹/₂″. c. 250. From the Via Salaria. Lateran Museum, Rome

In funerary sculpture too, Christian art of the third century took over pre-Christian themes and revivified them with new interpretations. With Plotinus there had come a philosophical religion of immortality and this was associated with a popular version of the same philosophy disseminated by wandering teachers. Where these ideas prevailed, a favorite funerary motif was the group of believers listening to their teacher. The transition to a strictly Christian funerary art and the final transformation into Christian symbolism of the two principal themes—the watchful shepherd and the philosopher with his disciples—were very gradual processes, so gradual, indeed, that we still cannot say with certainty which of the approximately 250 surviving sarcophagi from Rome's Via Salaria belonged to Christians. The familiar group of the philosopher with his disciples—male and female groups—confronts us on other sarcophagi much like this one, yet on them we see that, instead of the shepherd carrying a lamb, there is a gate, known to us from other examples as the gateway to the realm of the dead. The fact that the gateway is now, in the example above, replaced by the symbol of salvation, the Good Shepherd, and by the *orant* figure, suggests that this is a Christian sarcophagus, especially since this combination is to be seen many times over on a series of simpler tombs. We may certainly take it for granted that this is symbolic imagery, but we know too little about the concepts of the Early Christian world to be able to grasp its full import. Recent researches have been able to trace the origins of the coupling of the *orant* and the Good Shepherd to the doctrine of the twin virtues which was held in late Antiquity. The female *orant* personified *Pietas* (meek piety and devoutness), and the good shepherd personified *Philanthropia* (love of one's neighbor). Both virtues could be acquired from the study of philosophy. If this is accepted, there is no difficulty about assigning the Via Salaria sarcophagi to the realm of Christian art, and all the themes and symbols are explicable in the light of our knowledge of ideas current in late classical times.

Trough-shaped sarcophagus with *Orant*, Philosopher, and the Good Shepherd. Marble, 23¹/₄ x 85⁷/₈″. Third century. Santa Maria Antica, Rome ▶

The theme which combines the Philosopher or Teacher, the praying figure (*orant*), and the Good Shepherd on this sarcophagus from Santa Maria Antica must clearly be seen in a Christian context. On the right, near the Shepherd carrying the lamb, the baptism of Christ in the Jordan is shown. John the Baptist appears in the guise of one of those itinerant cynic philosophers encountered so many times on pre-Christian tombs. Much space is given on the left side, near the *orant,* to the story of the saving of Jonah, and the main scene shows the prophet resting in the shade of the gourd vine.

The Baptism must be understood here not as a scene from the life of Jesus, but as testimony that by baptism the Christian is redeemed, and that his individuality is unique. Through the rite of baptism the symbolic world of the pagans is redirected to a new meaning that tells of the true philosophy, the true faith, and the true love of mankind, without which there can be no promise of the salvation to which Christ alluded when He foretold His Resurrection on the third day. Jonah was a favorite figure for the Christian affirming his belief in salvation. In the imperishable and evergreen foliage of the gourd vine, which became the symbol of everlasting bliss, Jonah reposes in the form of the comely youth Endymion, a figure borrowed from pagan art by the Christian artist. The Endymion of mythology was the youthful son of Zeus, and to him that god had granted the gifts of eternal youth and eternal sleep; thus inevitably he came to play an essential and significant role in ancient funerary art.

The scenes depicted on the sarcophagus are placed in an idealized bucolic landscape which is only loosely related to the figures in it. For they are not a series of separate scenes from a single story, but are edifying examples. We find the same sort of thing in the Early Christian paradigmatic prayer which enumerated the great events of the Passion and Resurrection of Christ as precedents for the salvation everyone expected for himself. Such events as the saving of Jonah and of Daniel in the lions' den, or the miracle of Moses striking water from the rock, serve a similar purpose: they illustrate the need for baptism and the certainty of salvation. So it is manifest that at this period the message of an artistic composition could be as ambiguous as the meanings of the various figures in it. For there was still no known canon that had to be obeyed and there were still many varied influences and pressures at work.

Shepherd and Flock. Detail from a sarcophagus. Third or fourth century. Museo delle Terme, Rome

Grape Harvest with Statuettes of the Good Shepherd (detail). Marble, height 28³/₈″. Fourth century. From the Catacomb of ▶
Praetextatus. Lateran Museum, Rome

The theme of the Good Shepherd, so much liked by artists of the later years of Antiquity, furnishes an example of how easily ill-considered interpretations can lead to a complete misunderstanding of Early Christian imagery. It seems reasonable, however, to think here of the parable of the Good Shepherd who brings the lost lamb back to the fold. Consequently, there has been a tendency to take every such representation as an example of Early Christian art. But in these two cases, there is absolutely no justification for seeing a Christian meaning. The shepherd leaning on his staff as he guards his flock (facing page) is simply a rustic figure; later on, such a scene would quite naturally attract a Christian interpretation, to oust the Orpheus meaning. Even in the time of Theodosius the shepherd was by no means a Christian symbol beyond all doubt.

The *Grape Harvest* sarcophagus also shows three shepherds, one of them bearded. To associate these with Christ is to be totally misled, especially since the figures of the shepherds stand on pedestals and can therefore be taken to be statues in a vineyard. There must indeed be some close relationship linking shepherd, grape gathering, and sarcophagus, but this has not yet been satisfactorily explained.

Orant. Detail from a marble sarcophagus. Early third century. Torlonia Museum, Rome

Daniel in the Lions' Den. ▶ Detail of a sarcophagus from below San Paolo Fuori le Mura, Rome, with scenes of the Old and New Testaments. Marble. Second quarter of fourth century. Lateran Museum, Rome

"Oh God, save me as Thou didst once save Daniel from the den of lions," was the prayer of Early Christian communities. This is why the Early Christian artist portrayed Daniel as an *orant,* a beseecher, praying in the lions' den for deliverance just as the Christians prayed. In Saint Paul's Epistle to the Hebrews, a whole list of such precedents is set out, and common to all of them was faith as a "sure and certain hope." By faith, Noah and Isaac were saved; by faith, the children of Israel were led out of Egypt and through the Red Sea; and by faith, the lions' mouths were shut and the violence of the fire was quenched. Almost all of the great number of Old Testament scenes, shown on sarcophagi or painted in the catacombs, bore testimony to the strength of faith and to the *pietas* which found embodiment in the *orant* and utterance in the prayer of early Christians.

As in the Jonah scene, the story of preservation from death is presented in full. Daniel has prevailed over the lions to which he had been cast and appears as master over the animals, like Orpheus, and like the heraldic figure of the Lord of the Animals frequently represented in Antiquity. Strangely, this group (and only this one) stands on a plinthlike support, as did the Good Shepherd on the *Grape Harvest* sarcophagus.

Eusebius, Bishop of Caesarea (the fourth-century ecclesiastical historian), wrote, "And there by a spring in the middle of the market place was the figure of the Good Shepherd so well known to those versed in the Holy Scriptures; also Daniel surrounded by lions, cast in bronze, and overlaid with lustrous platings (?) of gold." We have already seen in the *Grape Harvest* sarcophagus from the Catacomb of Praetextatus that the Good Shepherd in stat-

The Good Shepherd. Marble statuette. Fourth century. Lateran Museum, Rome

Sarcophagus, with the Good ▶ Shepherd and lions' heads. Marble. Fourth century. Roman. The Louvre, Paris

ue form is not necessarily a Christian figure. The statuette shown here belongs to a series of more than thirty surviving, and of these, not a single one can confidently be related to Christian belief. We learn from literary sources that in pagan art similar representations of *Philanthropia* were common and were even in use as ornaments for tableware. The fluted or strigilated sarcophagi also have a distinct association with the pagan way of life.

Again (see below) we are concerned with the grape harvest. Scholars have long been aware that the strigilated trough- or vat-shaped sarcophagi with lions' head adornments derive from the Roman trough, the *alveus,* in which the wine treaders crushed the grapes with their feet (Klauser and Altmann). How the shepherd came into the decoration is still not explained. However, we are reminded of examples of statues which in later times were essentially Christian. There is early evidence for this view, for in the baptismal prayer in the Acts of Thomas, Christ is addressed thus, "Guard them from the wolves when Thou leadest them to Thy pastures; give them to drink from Thine ambrosial spring with its waters which never grow cloudy and never run dry, O Thou who art the Lord and the true Good Shepherd." Here the ritual of baptism, the *philanthropia* of Christ, and his role as Saviour (Latin and Greek *soter*) are so closely associated that the shepherd of the pagans and of the Christian parables is one and the same image. The way is clear now for the King-Shepherd, for the Basileus of the mosaic in the Galla Placidia mausoleum, for that "Holy Shepherd and King" of whom the contemporary Peter Chrysologus of Ravenna speaks in his homilies.

CONSTANTINE AND THEODOSIUS: CHRISTIAN ART IN ITALY

In the year 292, the Emperor Diocletian established the Tetrarchy with the object of reconciling the claims of the Eastern and Western Empires and uniting both the military and civil powers under overriding control from above. To the two "Augusti," Diocletian and Maximian, the eastern residing in Nicomedia and the western in Milan, were subordinated the two "Caesars," Galerius and Constantius Chlorus. These four rulers are portrayed in the porphyry group, certainly of about the year 300, which now stands on the south side of

the facade of Saint Mark's in Venice. This work is now considered to be the first example of Byzantine art. It is a product of the epoch in which the East was demanding equal rights with the Roman-Italian or Western Empire and was intent on making manifest their equal status in authority.

The raw material for this sculpture came from the east, from the quarries of the "Mons Porphyreticus" in Egypt. Later Byzantine artists considered that, because of its beauty as well as its costliness, porphyry was the best material for portrait sculptures in imperial buildings. The stylistic departure from Greco-Roman art, which had prevailed during the recent "renaissance" under the Emperor Gallienus, was a development of the use of porphyry for sculpture in the place where it was found. Even so, there is some harking back to the hieratic and inflexible forms which bore the stamp of characteristically barbarian and provincial artistic canons of the times of the warrior-emperors.

The persecutions of Christians in the later years of the Tetrarchy from 303 to 311 inevitably stifled production of Christian works of art.

Diocletian and His Co-Regents. Group of Tetrarchs. Porphyry, height $51^{1/8}''$. From Constantinople. South side of facade of Saint Mark's, Venice

Supposed portrait bust of Constantine the Great. Chalcedony, total height 7⅞". Beginning of fourth century. Cabinet des Médailles, Paris

After Constantine the Great's victory at the Milvian Bridge in 312, Christianity was declared to be the state religion by the Edict of Milan (313); and with this new official religion to sustain him, Constantine began his task of strengthening the imperial authority which was fast disintegrating. The Empire, now comprising all of Europe and the Mediterranean lands, established its new capital in the east, naming it Constantinople in honor of Constantine. He also revived the former imperial title and role of *Pontifex Maximus* and the Cross became the symbol of sovereign authority.

The small chalcedony bust, made for some long-forgotten purpose, is that of a Christian *imperator* of Constantine's time. Not only the characteristic delineation of the Roman *princeps augustus,* but also the noble and court art of carving in stone, both of these perfected in late classical times, seem to have come into their own again here.

Double solidus of Helena Augusta. Gold, 4½ oz. Struck in Ticinum (now Pavia). Cabinet des Médailles, Paris

Coin of Constantine with the *labarum*. Cabinet des Médailles, Paris

The *labarum* (military standard) with the sign of the Cross under which Constantine is supposed to have won his victory at the Milvian Bridge became the imperial banner, and Constantine's son, Constantius II, continued to be associated with it in his portraits. The dynasty of Constantine made use of the coinage for conveying Christian ideas: in particular the large medals or medallions, given as rewards to subordinates, have the symbol of the Christian reigning dynasty near the Emperor's head on the obverse side. The features of Helena, Constantine, and Constantius are well known to us, thanks to the coiners' art. We recognize the Emperor enthroned and haloed or seated in a war chariot with *nikes* (goddesses of victory) bearing his victor's laurels. As the process of Christianization advanced it is the hand of God, the *dextera Domini,* which proffers the wreath—a feature we have come to associate with the martyrs' cult. The imperial triumph is also equated with the Christian martyrs' victory over death and hell. The sons of Constantine, Constantine II, Constantius II, and Constans, developed a strong identification of the imperial triumph with divine majesty.

Constans as consul in a triumphal chariot. Gold medallion, diameter 18⁷/₈″.
Struck in Antioch in 339, 342, or 346. Münzkabinett, State Museums, Berlin

The need to make a splendid impression was a great concern of the reigning house, where imperial majesty was supposed to pass from father to son. The claim to total sovereignty and the claim (deriving from the symbol of the Cross) to be God's representative on earth demanded a monumental scale of expression. Constantine had a gigantic statue of himself placed in front of his basilica in Rome, of which only the head and a few fragments remain. The so-called *Colossus of Barletta,* over sixteen feet in height, represents a Christian emperor of the Constantinian succession, possibly Marcianus or Heraclius. The size of the figure and the severity of facial expression elevate him far above his fellow men—a place to which he is entitled by virtue of his office as well as by his personal qualities. Christian art is well on its way to becoming an official art representing the essence of the state. This was the principle, dictating both form and content, which Byzantine art in its full flowering under Justinian embraced.

Colossus of Barletta. Bronze, height 16′ 9″. Dated variously between 450 and 629. Barletta Cathedral

Pignatara Gate. Ruins of the mausoleum of Saint ▶ Helena. Beginning of fourth century, Rome

Just as the pre-Christian *imperator* had been responsible for temple building, so church building belonged to the responsibilities of the imperial house. The official church of the bishop in Rome, as in Constantinople, stood close to the imperial palace. Even at the beginning of the fourth century, the ruling house of Constantine was building churches with connotations of the imperial cult all over the Empire.

Besides the parish churches and the bishop's churches, there were the *memoriae,* which had their own special function. André Grabar, the French art historian, who devoted much of his research to these memorial precincts for martyrs and the early church fathers, once described them very strikingly as "vast reliquaries." Naturally, members of the imperial house were numbered among those whom the Church honored in such a way. Constantine not only had Christ's burial place in Jerusalem rebuilt in memory of his mother Helena; he also, and probably employing the same architect, built a mausoleum in Rome as a monument to her.

The basic tomb form was the rotunda. This was the shape of the ancient heroes' *heroa* (part sanctuary and part mausoleum). Constantine respected this tradition but frequently associated the monument with a building intended for services, as often as not a basilica, thereby ensuring that the tomb building was linked with places associated with the most highly venerated martyrs. To be buried *ad martyros* was the aspiration of every Christian. The memorials to martyrs of high degree were the basilicas themselves.

San Giovanni in Laterano, Rome. Fresco attributed to Gaspard Poussin or Gaspard Dughet. Seventeenth century. San Martino ai Monti, Rome

The great basilicas which Constantine created in Rome have all but vanished. On a site adjoining his imperial palace in Rome, the Lateran, Constantine built the first *cathedral* (bishop's church), dedicated to Saint John, now San Giovanni in Laterano. Like the Church of the Nativity in Bethlehem, a foundation of Saint Helena, the Lateran cathedral is still fairly well preserved. As befitted the church of the bishop in Rome, San Giovanni in Laterano had a nave with four aisles separated by arcades resting on pedestaled marble columns. We learn from a fresco in San Martino ai Monti that a fairly wide transept was added later and the central nave was extended to terminate in a projecting apse rising to the same height. The church was adorned with precious materials—columns of porphyry, marble coverings, and mosaics on a gold ground. Over the arcades was a frieze which was separated from the clerestory by a continuous entablature. The fresco, attributed to Gaspard Poussin, is one of a series of representations of the first great Roman cathedrals. It shows the state of the basilica before the rebuilding of 1650.

Saint Peter's, Rome. Fresco showing Early Christian structure. Seventeenth century. San Martino ai Monti, Rome

We are well informed as to the original appearance of the basilica of Saint Peter in Rome thanks to the many detailed accounts and to building surveys made during the great rebuilding at the time of the High Renaissance. Tiberius Alphanus has left us an accurately measured ground plan and exact details of the building about to be superseded. The church was probably first consecrated in 330; over the grave of the Prince of the Apostles rose the supreme building of Western Christianity.

The wall painting in San Martino ai Monti shows above the colonnades in the nave a monumental architrave carrying the walls supporting the roof. The *confessio,* or shrine, in the middle of the narrow transept was emphasized by the two great round-arched openings to the choir and to the nave.

San Paolo Fuori le Mura was built over the burial place of the other great Apostle, Saint Paul, in much the same way as Saint Peter's. The five-aisled basilica was the characteristic Early Christian church form. The great bishops' churches were nearly all built to this plan.

In pre-Christian times, the basilica was a kind of large meeting hall used for legal and official business; it had itself evolved from a Greek public courtyard of assembly, also used as a court of justice and an exchange. The various adaptations of this basic plan for a colonnaded building, to be seen in Christian architecture in many parts of the world and still made use of in our own day, represent the most influential artistic achievement of the age of Constantine. Its fundamental forms already existed in Roman civic architecture and needed to draw only for detail on the heritage of the eastern provinces, Christianized earlier. In Constantine's lifetime the basilican plan was so much taken for granted in both the east and the west that he was able to use it for the church of the Holy Sepulcher in Jerusalem, just as he would have done for a similar structure of similar, if less exalted, significance in Rome or its environs.

When Constantine achieved sole sovereignty in Rome after his defeat of Maxentius at the Milvian Bridge he took over a partly constructed building, the Basilica Nova, from his adversary and had it turned into his own imperial basilica. This accomplished, he began the building of his great Christian basilicas.

Ruins of the Basilica Nova, Rome. Fourth century

The eastern Christian communities, especially in Syria, had their own tradition of roofed-over assembly halls with the roof often spanning a clearly cruciform ground plan. In early years such secular buildings were taken over as they were for the practice of the Christian cult. The surviving remnants of the fourth century in this region give us a good idea of the variations in this type of structure. To some extent the Syrian basilica was influenced by Constantinople and to some extent it developed, along independent lines, elements which had originated in the capital. The Syrians were particularly interested in the division of the nave into several distinct sections. Two arches would be united in an arcade under a huge superimposed arch. Large projecting piers or other supports divided these arches spatially from one another. Thus there arose here what is known to western architects as a "tie." The inspiration for this architectural form, a development essential to the evolution of the vault and the cupola, certainly came from the East; there is also a clear example of it in North Africa in the fourth-century basilica of Tebessa (Algeria).

The basilica of Sergiopolis (Syria) probably dates from the sixth century and illustrates the principle, developed under Byzantine influence, of marking the main aisle off spatially into subdivisions with great angular piers, between which were fitted arcades resting on columns.

Santa Costanza, Rome. Above: exterior. Right: interior

When Constantine declared Constantinople the capital city, he initiated in the east of his empire an energetic and comprehensive building program in the holy places of Christianity. For the sepulcher of Christ he erected a great *memoria* (see page 33). We can only surmise what its appearance must have been in his day—probably a circular building attached to a basilica. At the same time he erected near the basilica of Sant'Agnese in Rome the mausoleum for members of the imperial family known today as Santa Costanza, which was the burial place of his daughter Constantia (d. 354), probably built within her lifetime and originally planned as a baptistery. He himself wished to be buried in his circular tomb in his capital, Constantinople. The building of Santa Costanza develops a little more the idea of the circular *memoria* by raising the actual cupola on an arcade of paired columns encircled by a barrel-vaulted ambulatory which takes the thrust of the cupola. Thus, plentifully flooded with daylight (and originally decorated with mosaics), its interior has a less ponderous effect, and the whole rotunda has an air of increased breadth and splendor. The somewhat greater width of the middle arches serves to mark a central axis; this led not to an altar, but to the porphyry sarcophagus itself, erected within the altar recess upon its plinth, of Constantia who thus still held court in death.

Christ and Saint Peter. Niche mosaic. Fourth or early fifth century. From Santa Costanza, Rome

The mosaics of Santa Costanza between the windows of the rotunda, on the ambulatory walls, in the bays, and in the decoration of the dome have vanished save for a few scanty remnants. We know from Renaissance drawings that the walls were all lavishly adorned with mosaics. On the vaults of the two semicircular side bays two scenes survive which have direct reference to the founding of the Christian Church. On one side, God delivers the Commandments to Moses; on the other, Christ gives Peter the care of the Church. This juxtaposition is, of course, intended to make the point that, in the *traditio legis* ("the handing down of the Law"), an event of the same magnitude as the Old Testament delivery of the Ten Commandments to Moses is happening to Peter.

The mosaics of the ambulatory, both in form and in content, have close kinship with Roman floor mosaics of pre-Christian times. Over a white background, vine tendrils, animals, and various shapes and objects combine in fluent and lighthearted ornament. Trailing branches with perching birds, grape clusters, *putti* (young boys, often cupids) playing or helping with the grape harvesting and wine pressing have much of the gaiety of the Early Christian catacomb paintings. They make no unmistakably Christian allusions, however, and can have had no close relationship with the Biblical scenes which once decorated the rotunda, or the scenes dealing with church history in the bays. At least we may conjecture, from the surviving mosaics in the bays, that those are of a later date than the decorative mosaics on the ambulatory vault.

Decorative mosaic in the ambulatory. Fourth century. Santa Costanza, Rome

Neither the sarcophagus of the Emperor's daughter Constantia in the royal mausoleum, nor that of his mother Helena, testify unequivocally to an acceptance of Christianity. The grape-harvesting putti encircled in interlacing medallions appeared so often that they may indeed be taken as Christian allegories, but we do not need to assume that they sprang directly from any Christian doctrine. It is a matter of an officially accepted art form traditional in the old workshops and in their fixed range of figures and subjects. For the porphyry sarcophagi, however, we must suggest Egyptian manufacture.

The pageant of the seasons was a favorite theme of pagan funerary and mosaic art. There was a definite link with notions concerning death, prevailing in late classical times, which could thus be given a Christian connotation and which were obviously adaptable to the decoration of Christian churches. A governor named Olympiodorus wrote Nilus, who lived as a hermit on Mount Sinai, saying that he wanted to build a magnificent church and to adorn it with hunting, fishing, and similar scenes, and with wild animals as well as a thousand crosses. The reply was that he should rather content himself with just one cross, for pictures of hunting scenes were childish folly. Such scenes as were depicted should edify those ignorant of Holy Writ and should exhort them to follow it. Here we are at the starting point of Christian iconography.

Sarcophagus of Constantia, daughter of Constantine the Great, d. 354. Porphyry, 88⅝ × 91¾ × 61″. From Santa Costanza. Vatican Museums, Rome

Via Crucis sarcophagus. Marble, 23¹/₄ x 79¹/₂″. Middle of the fourth century. Probably from the Catacomb of Domitilla. Lateran Museum, Rome

The establishment of Christianity as the state religion brought a new influence on the development of Christian iconography in several ways. Now that the official Church and the State were one and undivided, there came a new and universal freedom in the illustration of Christian themes. Suggestions such as those of Nilus could now be carried out. Christ was not only presented as a symbol but was shown in person in New Testament episodes. There is a whole series of fourth-century sarcophagi with a common theme. As far as both the form and the arrangement of the various scenes were concerned, it was not long before clearly differentiated fundamental types began to emerge. There were sarcophagi with friezes, bays, arcades, and buttresses. Sarcophagi with two registers gave opportunities for a greater number of holy themes.

The *Via Crucis*—the "Way of the Cross of Christ"—is the theme of the sarcophagus shown above, with events of Christ's Passion framed between pillars. These created a definite sequence of episodes, the significance of which (as in the case of many other sarcophagi) is revealed in the area between the two central pillars. The culminating episode here one might reasonably expect to be the Crucifixion, but we have instead a victor's wreath of laurels and the monogram of Christ set above a cross. This, however, is still in accordance with one of the most persistent pictorial schemes of the ancient world. The weapons of a defeated enemy were hung over a wooden framework made in the shape of a cross which bore an escutcheon with the victor's name; close by, perhaps in fetters and perhaps lamenting, there stood or sat soldiers in the service of the conquered enemy. In terms of this standard symbolism, Christ's death on the Cross on the *Passion* sarcophagi is transformed into the victory of the Resurrection. The Cross is His *Tropaion,* the banner under which He fought to win the victor's crown. Thus His bearing of it becomes a triumphal procession in which it is borne along as a standard or banner. The crown of thorns becomes an honor associated with a triumph, a wreath of victory laurels. When supreme authority, in the person of Pilate washing his hands of all responsibility, shows its own inadequacy, then Christ appears and those who seized Him become His guard of honor.

The death of Christ has furnished Christians with their greatest symbol in the shape of the instrument of that death. That is why the sarcophagus is an appropriate place for it, since it is the Cross which transforms the Christian's death likewise into his triumph. Here the Elysian serenity of Early Christian art is superseded by the conventions of victory derived from all the new trappings of statecraft and war, the idea of resplendent triumph replacing that of passive bliss.

Pillared sarcophagus with Christ and the Apostles. Marble, height 31¹/₈″. Third quarter of fourth century. Saint Peter's, ▶ Rome (until 1954 in the Lateran)

Portrayals of the crucified Christ were avoided in Early Christian art, but Christ was introduced into the center panel of a sarcophagus as Redeemer if, through the details depicted around Him, He could thereby be exalted. To this end the time-honored stylization of the cosmos was used: Christ reigns over the firmament on His heavenly throne with Apostles standing on either side of Him, those Apostles to whom the continuation of His work on earth had been entrusted. This is the risen Christ who through His Passion, generally depicted in the outer fields between the pillars, has established the Church. In our illustration, the right-hand side shows Pilate washing his hands and the left shows an appropriate Old Testament scene: the sacrifice of Isaac. This juxtaposition implies that Man—or more exactly, the person lying in the sarcophagus—will be redeemed by the sacrifice of Christ just as Isaac was by the sacrifice of the lamb. This is confirmed by another of Christ's actions: the giving of the new dispensation to Peter. Such a scene is called the *traditio legis,* from which the Christian Church derives its claim to have received its Commandments from Christ, Lord of the Universe like the Yahweh of the Old Testament, just as Moses received the Tablets of the Law from Yahweh Himself.

Most of the sarcophagi were probably made, classified according to the groups of themes most in demand, as stock items in the workshops. Often the heads on them were not supplied until later, when likenesses of the deceased were made—usually a husband and wife. Two brothers are interred in this sarcophagus: the customary procedure was not quite appropriate here but nevertheless it was used. The two masculine portraits in the *clipeus* (shell-like recess bearing portraits) are rendered as if they were a married couple. Even the toga of the man on the left is arranged in the kind of pleats that make it recognizable as a woman's garment.

Sarcophagus of the Two Brothers. Tomb for two people. Marble, 44¹/₂ x 83⁷/₈″. Second third of fourth century. From a cemetery at San Paolo Fuori le Mura. Lateran Museum, Rome. Facing page: detail

In the two registers, in no particular sequence and with no formal connection, scenes from the Old and New Testaments jostle with one another. On both sides of the portraits are Old Testament scenes, illustrating God's Commandments, where Yahweh manifests Himself through the hand presenting the Tablets of the Law and forbids Abraham to sacrifice Isaac. Near this presentation of the Commandments we again see the *traditio legis* to Peter. On this sarcophagus Peter now takes on a significant role, appearing as a second Moses, which accounts for his appearing also in the lower row of figures in the episode of the miracle of striking water from the rock. Scholars have not yet succeeded in explaining all the episodes connected with Peter shown on this sarcophagus. Moreover, coherence and continuity are utterly destroyed by the interpolation of salvation and miracle episodes. Daniel in the lions' den appears between two scenes involving Saint Peter, and on the lower register to the right, Christ is seen miraculously restoring sight to the blind and multiplying the loaves and fishes. This tomb represents the zenith of Early Christian art in the middle of the fourth century. It is illuminating for the position of Early Christian art, that this crowning work should be a stock item that anyone could order.

Christ is shown here as a handsome young man. Supple folds of the garments drape the clearly identifiable bodily forms which stand out in almost full relief from the background. On the facing page, the majestic figure of Christ at the tomb of Lazarus (upper register) lends a contrapuntal grace to the composition. The soldier debating with Peter (lower register) shows surprise and astonishment. All the groups are variously and rhythmically articulated.

Sarcophagus of Junius Bassus, d. 359. Pentelic marble, length 95⁵/₈″. Vaults of Saint Peter's, Rome

We know the name and the rank of the individual who commissioned this most important work in the middle of the fourth century, and we know too the date at which it was put to its intended use—which must be fairly close to the date of its creation. In an inscription Junius Bassus, who died at the age of forty-two, is identified as Prefect of the city of Rome. The date of his death is given (according to the chronology of that era which is based on consulships) as August 25, 359. The word "died" is interpreted as "went to God" (*iit ad Deum*). As opposed to the *Sarcophagus of the Two Brothers,* the transfigured Christ is shown in the middle of the upper row of figures as Lord of the Heavens as He hands over the Commandments. The seizing of Christ, the arrest of Peter, Paul's road to martyrdom: these are the three *viae dolorosae* by which the three figures in the middle scenes came at last to heavenly glory. As unsullied as Christ was, when on Palm Sunday he rode into Jerusalem, so shall the dead man "go to God." The stylistic beauty of the *Two Brothers* sarcophagus is here developed to the highest degree of refinement. Pentelic marble, richly translucent, is smoothly worked and polished. The arrangement of the separate groups, usually of three figures, in the panels separated by pillars is such as to create a dense concentration of individual images, a feature peculiar to this sarcophagus, the nearest equivalent of it being the concentrated compactness of the Greek metopes. Christian art at this level, in the quality and dignity of its productions, returns to the artistic tradition of Antiquity, applying the Apollonian ideal of beauty to its representation of Christ's majesty.

Christ's Entry into Jerusalem. Detail from the sarcophagus of Junius Bassus ▶

49

Christt the Teacher. Detail from ▶ the Milan "city-gate" sarcophagus

As the fourth century progressed, the pillared type of sarcophagus evolved in such a way that the pillars assumed architectural groupings with towers, passages, and gateways; the name of "city-gate" sarcophagi has been given to this new form. Two thus classified have so many features in common that a close connection may be assumed.

The facade almost invariably shows, below the centrally placed gateway, Christ with Peter and Paul, the handing on of the Commandments, or Christ preaching a sermon to the Apostles—a scene which is to be interpreted as the dispatching of the Apostles on their mission. Most of these sarcophagi have ornamental patterns on the pedestal, as often as not a continuous scroll of vines or tendrils; on the front of the cornice, as well as a portrait of the deceased or perhaps a plaque with an inscription, there is an iconographic scheme exclusive to that particular tomb. The other sides of the cornice carry Christian symbols, especially Christ's own emblem. There are sculptures on all four sides of these sarcophagi.

The best-known example is the Milan "city-gate" sarcophagus, closely associated with the teachings of Saint Ambrose. All the themes translated into sculpture can be related to his preaching as it has come down to us. On the front and back of the tomb are episodes from the calling and ordaining of the Apostles. Christ presides as the *Princeps Apostolorum* ("Prince of the Apostles"). The two side panels are devoted to Christ's prophecies—for example, His Ascension as foretold in Elijah's ascent in the fiery chariot. On the cornice near the portraits of the couple laid to rest, the sculptures conform to a particularly strict program. Opposite the scene of the Three Magi worshiping is a scene showing the refusal of the Three Young Men in the Fiery Furnace to worship the king and their subsequent deliverance. The juxtaposition makes it clear that this is an allusion to the contrast between spiritual and worldly adoration. The fact that these scenes adjoin the portraits of the married couple makes them into a personal testament. It is as though the deceased are calling attention to how much their love for God surpasses their regard for worldly powers; they hope to be saved as the youths were saved from the fiery furnace.

The Good Shepherd. Marble statuette. End of third century. The Louvre, Paris

The young and personable Christ of the Milan "city-gate" sarcophagus is undoubtedly to be understood as representing in that scene the God of the Christians in His own person. In fourth-century art it was taken for granted that to portray a young man teaching was to portray Christ. It is also at this period that sculptured figures of Christ shown fully in the round were produced, but there was no development of them in the early art of the West once it had been christianized. In Byzantium itself they were extremely rare.

As for the small statuettes of the "good shepherd," it is not now possible to say with certainty that they represent Christ —it is only in the course of time that they have gathered such claims. Portrayals of Christ came to be almost exclusively associated in funerary art with the events of the Passion or the *traditio legis*, with

Christ the Teacher. Marble. Third–fourth century. Museo delle Terme, Rome

Christ shown as Redeemer and as Founder of the Church in accordance with sacred teachings.

This was also the time of the appearance of the youthful Christ, fair as Apollo, as we have seen Him on the Milan "citygate" sarcophagus and, indeed, in a closely related scene on the back of the same tomb, where he stands as a youthful figure almost face to face with a bearded Christ of the "philosopher" type. The range of sculptured figures in relief developed in the early years of Christian art is much as might be expected, but this art did not achieve the monumentality which ample architectural dimensions would require. Such a scale was for a long time confined to mural painters. It is possible, generally speaking, that the tombs of about the year 400, so rich in their iconography, are a reflection of the work of these painters.

The Brescia Lipsanotheca. Ivory, $8^5/8 \times 12^7/8''$. c. 360–70. Formerly in Santa Giulia, Brescia. Brescia Museum

Much use was made in classical times of the precious material ivory; we have examples in such large numbers of carved ivory from late Antiquity, dating from the middle of the fourth century, that we can work out their stylistic evolution. There is admittedly one circumstance that partially invalidates such a sequence —the fact that the ivories came from different workshops all over the Empire, for instance from Trier, Rome itself, Antioch, Alexandria, and Constantinople, among other places; it is impossible to attribute more than a few to this or that source. Ivory was used chiefly for diptychs (hinged tablets) and pyxes (sacramental vessels).

The Brescia Lipsanotheca. Above: detail of back, showing Peter rebuking Ananias and Sapphira. Below: front edge of lid, showing the young Christ between Apostles

The Brescia ivory casket or *Lipsanotheca* (reliquary) is decorated with figures in relief on all four sides and on the lid. For a long time the component pieces were fastened to a cross; when the cross was cleaned, the pieces were reassembled into their original casket form. On the larger surfaces, New Testament scenes are carved, and on the smaller, Old Testament episodes which, as we have seen with funerary art, are related to New Testament happenings. The lid is reserved for the Passion of Christ.

The rebuking of Ananias and Sapphira by Peter is shown in detail on the back panel of the casket. Its theme, the misappropriation of moneys belonging to the Church, and therefore to the Christian community, could be a hint as to the original purpose of the casket, especially since this scene is uncommon. On the front vertical edge of the lid are medallion portraits of Apostles with that of Christ in the middle; there Christ is shown, as elsewhere on the casket, as a beardless young man.

After Diocletian had divided imperial sovereignty among the two Augusti and the two Caesars (the Tetrarchy), Trier became the capital and seat of government of the Western Empire. After 287, Maximian (293) and Constantius Chlorus (293–305) resided there. The son of the latter, Constantine the Great, had Trier as his base until he established Constantinople. He had many buildings erected in Trier, fragments of which survive, and saw to the city's defenses (Porta Nigra). His mother Helena chose to live there also from time to time. Later it was the residence of Valentinian I (364–75) and his son Gratian (375–83). At this time Trier was also the center of spiritual life in the West. Naturally there must have been craftsmen with their workshops attached to the palace, as numerous finds seem to indicate. Research has established a connection with some such workshop in the case of the casket, or pyx, illustrated here, which was found in a village near Trier. The front shows the young Christ enthroned beneath a pillared arch, surrounded by Apostles. On the other side is Abraham's sacrifice. The scene with Christ and the Apostles reminds us in configuration and iconography of the impressive fourth-century sarcophagi. The "nobility" of the figure treatment suggests that this is a product of the second half of the fourth century, since then, as other ivories demonstrate, some of the ideals of classical Antiquity were taking on a new lease of life. Even in small ornamental features this revival is evident—the beautifully proportioned band of beading shows it, as well as the "astragal" molding around the upper rim.

On the London casket, a scheme of events already encountered in funerary art has been carried out, namely the events of Holy Week. The panels show Pilate washing his hands, the carrying of the Cross, the death of Judas, the crucifixion of Christ, the women at the sepulcher, and doubting Thomas. The figures are squat and thickset, the heads disproportionately large, the facial features emphatic. The approach to the human figure has nothing in common with that of the carver of the Trier pyx. The London casket, together with a whole group of ivories that includes the ivory diptych of the Lampardi family in Brescia Museum, and also the side panels of a five-part diptych in Paris and Berlin, has been dated to the year 420 and traced back to Upper Italy.

The Guards and the Women at the Tomb. One leaf of a diptych. Ivory, $12 \times 5^{1}/4''$. c. 400. From the Trivulzio Collection. Museum of the Castello Sforzesco, Milan

This diptych panel showing the women at Christ's sepulcher comes from the Trivulzio Collection. It belongs to the second half of the fourth century, and its bas-relief execution is striking. All the essentials are depicted in these two scenes, and yet the impression of spatial depth and of bodies seen fully in the round is perfectly convincing. We notice in the upper scene the diagonal line of the spear lying on the ground, a space-creating device, and in the lower scene the figure of the angel before the entrance to the Tomb portrayed with masterly skill in the classic seated position. Above, again, are the two guards bowed in weariness before a burial rotunda, over which are the symbols associated with Saint Luke and Saint Matthew. The lower scene relates more explicitly to the Biblical event. Before the door, which is decorated with patterns in relief and let into a brick wall representing the Tomb, a seated angel is telling the women that Christ has risen. An ornamental frame surrounds the scene, a frame seen also on the tablets of the *Nicomachi* and *Symmachi* (see page 66) and likewise furnishing evidence of classical tendencies in the fourth century.

The same episode of the women at the sepulcher is represented on the Munich ivory in a more literal version of the Biblical text—the guards and the women approaching the sepulcher are no longer the subjects of two opposed pictures separated by an ornamental frame, but are linked in a single scene that includes Christ's Ascension. This fact, and also the general proportions, justify the surmise that here we have the middle tablet of a five-part diptych.

As the three Marys draw near to the tomb, shown here as an intricate architectural structure adorned with sculptures in niches and with tondi, enabling us to make certain deductions concerning contemporary tastes in building, Christ ascends heavenward. The hand of God grasps Christ's right hand and two Apostles witness the scene. Particularly effective on this ivory is the molding of form, as though in a painting, which serves to detach the figures both in the sky and on the earth from their backgrounds, and the successful suggestion of the interplay of light and shadow resulting from the use of an openwork technique for the trees.

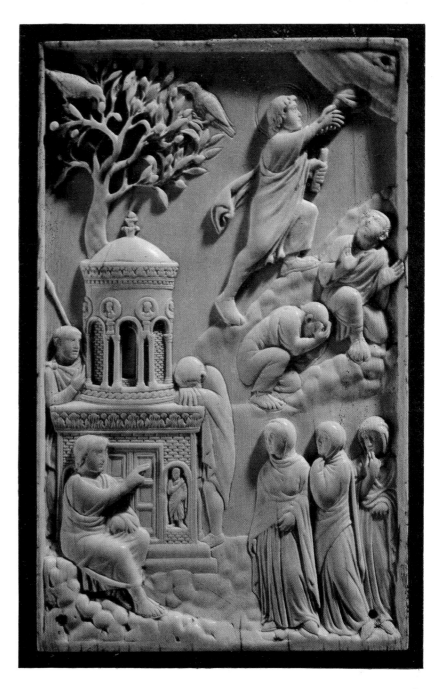

The Women at the Tomb and The Ascension. Ivory, $7^3/_8 \times 4^5/_8''$. Bayerisches Nationalmuseum, Munich

The small ivory plaque in the Museum at Dijon shows the *Collegium Sacrum,* the Apostles surrounding Christ, who is enthroned centrally in the composition and is larger than all the other figures. There are curtains behind Him gathered into folds; Peter and Paul are to His right and left. The Apostles are shown in reversed perspective: those in the foreground are the smallest and those nearest to Christ the largest, a convention which gives prominence to the three most exalted. On the table is a circular container with eight scrolls, the Gospels and the books of the Prophets.

The ivory from the cathedral treasury at Milan (facing page) probably comprised, with its companion leaf, a luxurious cover for a Bible or a gospel book. In the fifth and sixth centuries the rich and ingeniously decorated book cover was one of the most sought-after productions of the artist-craftsman. The front cover shown here has in its central panel the haloed Lamb, encircled with a garland, standing under an entablature supported by two columns. The surrounding panels show New Testament scenes, and those in great pro-

fusion. Particularly significant is the inclusion of episodes involving the Virgin Mary—the Annunciation and the Purification. From the way the Annunciation is represented, it appears that the Apocryphal Gospel of James was the source: the prologue to the actual Annunciation in this source is also included. In both scenes, Mary is regally arrayed. The bottom panel, showing Herod's Massacre of the Innocents in Bethlehem, is colored by palace ceremonial. The top panel shows the Nativity, a subject that was treated pictorially as early as the fourth century. However, it was not until after the year 431, the date of the Council of Ephesus when Mary was accepted as *Theotokos* or Mother of God, that the birth of Christ became an important feature in Christian iconography. Here the event is still shown, as was usual in Early Christian art, in a setting with hints of an architectural background. The Byzantine artists of the sixth century were the first to show the grotto of the Nativity. In the upper two medallions are the symbols of the Evangelists Matthew and Luke, and in the lower two they themselves are portrayed as men.

Collegium Sacrum. Christ and the Apostles. Ivory. Fifth century. Museum, Dijon

Leaf of a diptych with five panels. Second half of fifth century. Ivory, 14³/₄ × 11″. Cathedral treasury, Milan

Lionbaiting in an Arena. Diptych. Ivory, height 12³/₄″, width of each panel 4¹/₈″. Probably Roman. The Hermitage, Leningrad

The purpose of these two plaques showing lionbaiting in its various aspects is unknown to us. Possibly they were writing tablets. The surfaces, which have no noticeable subdivisions, are decorated all over with lions and lion fighters, much as they are to be seen in mosaic floors. Both tablets have a narrow frame of ovoid beads and bars. The men wear a tunic with a protective garment over it which in some cases covers one arm. This garb may indicate that the subject here is a circus entertainment. Since the consular figure appearing in scenes on consular diptychs is known to have been an organizer of circus performances, it is conceivable that these two plaques may also have been parts of a consular diptych.

Like ivory, glass was a highly esteemed material for the smaller works of art. It may even have been considered superior because of the difficulties inherent in its manufacture and because of its fragility. Before the invention of glassblowing, glass objects, including beads, were opaque: we know this from early Egyptian finds and those of other cultures. It was not until the technique of glassblowing was discovered that attempts were made to purify molten glass and render it transparent. Naturally, coloring agents came to be added, for instance pulverized semiprecious stones, to give it a gleaming tint. The *Situla Pagana* ("heathen bucket"), the pail from pagan times in the cathedral treasury of Saint Mark's, Venice, is one of the most precious of those to have survived. It is a *diatretum,* that is to say, the basic glass vessel is overlaid with a vitreous network —in this case, only halfway up the sides, the upper half being decorated with a band of mounted men. At the moment we know of only eight *diatreta* in a good state of preservation. The last to come to light, a particularly fine example, was found in Cologne as recently as 1960.

Situla Pagana. Pail or wine bucket with hunting scenes. Lightly tinted glass. Fourth century. Cathedral treasury, Saint Mark's, Venice

Family portrait. Gold glass, diameter 2⅜″. Fourth century. From 1437 in cloister of Santa Giulia; now in Museo Civico, Brescia

Bowl. Polished glass, diameter 8³/₄″. Fourth century. Römisch-Germanisches Museum, Cologne

The so-called "gold-glass" objects represent a variation in the art of working with glass and employ both glass-working and metalworking techniques. A sheet of gold leaf is laid between two sheets of glass after designs have either been painted on or incised into the gold leaf with a tool like a burin or etching needle. The portrait on gold glass illustrated here is let into a silver processional cross of the seventh century which is further ornamented with four miniatures, uncut stones, gems, and artificial jewels of glass paste. The effective combination and the high quality of the gold glass—most examples of this art form are far more primitive—suggest a palace or other courtly provenance. The personages portrayed could be (but there are other possibilities) Galla Placidia with her children Valentinian III and Honoria. An inscription refers to a Greek painter, "Boynneri Kerami."

This glass bowl with curving sides was found in an ossuary in the Cologne area, opened up in 1920, which yielded an exceptionally rich hoard of Antique glass. Coins of Maximian, who died in 310, were also found there. The bowl dates from the later years of the fourth century. It is made of greenish glass and is decorated with polished-glass ornaments. On the outside of the vessel (as also on the base) are three appliqué female heads with parted hair bound by a fillet. Between these, there are three hooked lugs which, since their ends are flattened, could have been used for picking up the bowl.

These two ivory leaves were for a time at the shrine of Bercharius who died in 675 at Montier-en-Der. According-ing to an inscription, he brought them back with him from the Holy Land. The leaf with the inscription NICOMACHORUM was acquired by the Cluny Museum, Paris, in 1860; the other, with the inscription SYMMACHORUM, by the Victoria and Albert Museum, London, in 1865. Both show pagan sacrificial rites. These pieces probably originated in Rome, where the families of Symmachus and Nicomachus were members of the senate. In their emphatic return to ancient pagan tradition and to the formal conventions associated with it they are proof that the strivings toward a revival of classical art, which mark the end of the fourth century, were supported in Rome at any rate by a distinguished non-Christian upper class.

Diptych of Stilicho and his wife Serena. Ivory, each leaf 12⅝ × 6¼". c. 400. Cathedral treasury, Monza

More or less contemporaneous with the *Symmachi* and *Nicomachi* leaves is the diptych of Stilicho and his wife Serena with their son Honorius, probably fashioned in Milan. Stilicho is seen gazing out at us here, dressed in a handsome *chlamys* or military mantle and with lance and shield. From the flat surface of the shield the double portrait of the Western and Eastern Emperors projects in high relief.

◀ Diptych of the *Nicomachi* and *Symmachi*. Ivory, each leaf 11½ × 5". c. 400. Left: Cluny Museum, Paris. Right: Victoria and Albert Museum, London

Consular diptych of the proconsul Rufius Probianus. Ivory. c.380. Staatsbibliothek, Berlin

The Projecta Casket. Silver, partially gilded. Detail of box showing portraits. c. 400. British Museum, London (see also p. 70)

The consular diptych of Probianus also illustrates an aspect of political life. Its resounding inscription informs us that we are looking at RUFIUS PROBIANUS V[IR] C[LARISSIMUS] VICARIUS URBIS RO- MAE ("Rufius Probianus, the illustrious, regent of the city of Rome"); it also acquaints us with the fact of his accession to office as consul. Probianus is portrayed twice over. Frames of interlaced palms divide the diptych into four areas. The consul, on his seat of office in the tribunal, is seen against architectural features drawn in perspective. In the left-hand leaf he has put aside the manuscript, in the right-hand one it lies unrolled on his knees. We read the opening words of the text, which are PROBIANE FLOREAS ("Probianus, may you flourish"). The consul indicates that he has assumed office by drawing a line with his stylus through his own name, signifying acceptance of the honor. In the lower halves officials acclaim him.

The *Projecta Casket* of embossed silver, partially gilded, is shown by its inscription to be a Christian work of art, in spite of the pagan scenes: SECUNDE ET PROJECTA VIVATIS IN CHRI[STO] ("Secundus and Projecta, may you live in Christ"). The couple are shown on the slanting lid framed in a wreath supported on each side by *putti*.

The Projecta Casket. Silver, partially gilded, 11 x 21⁷/₈″. c. 400. British Museum, London

The portraits on the lid and designs elsewhere on the box lead us to the conclusion that this was a bridal chest. On the front edge of the lid is Venus as goddess of love, flanked by tritons and nereids. On the two facing sides, to her left and right, we see the bride being conducted into a palace. In the middle of the arcade on the front of the box, the bride is busy at her dressing and servant girls are approaching from both sides with articles she needs, such as a cosmetics box and a looking glass. There are peacocks in the two outer- most arches, and in those on the other sides are female figures, probably servants, carrying vessels. The bridal chest was used for storing gifts and may be seen as a forerunner of the *cassoni* so much in demand during the Early and High Renaissance—chests or trunks covered with paintings of secular subjects, often the work of famous masters such as Botticelli, Uccello, and Andrea del Sarto.

Whereas numerous ivories, some of them precisely dated, have come down to us so that we are almost able to establish a reliable chronology for them, the history of metalwork remains very incomplete. Of course, we have to bear in mind that the intrinsic value of some metals and the ease with which such works could be melted down made them obvious booty for thieves and looters. We know from several sources, for instance, the *Liber Pontificalis* or "History of the Popes," that there must have been a huge number of metal objects which have since vanished. Questions of dating and of the associations between various centers and workshops are not easily settled when the evidence is so meager.

The *missorium* (dish) of the Emperor Theodosius I is an important object of the gold- and silversmith's art and in the history of metalworking. It bears a date and there is enough evidence for its provenance to be established. The inscription reads: D[OMINUS] N[OSTER] THEODOSIUS PERPET[UUS] AUG[US- TUS] OB DIEM FELICISSIMUM X ("Our lord Theodosius, for ever 'Augustus' [magnificent, noble] for the most auspicious day ten"). Since this Theodosius, because of his two co-rulers portrayed here, Arcadius

Missorium of Emperor Theodosius I. Silver, diameter 29″. 388. Royal Academy, Madrid

and Valentinian II, is bound to be Theodosius I, and since he was celebrating, in the year 388, the Festival of the Decennalia, his tenth anniversary as sovereign, we can take 388 as a definite date knowing that the "X" refers to that year. As for the provenance, we have the following two hints: at the time of his tenth anniversary, Theodosius was staying in Salonika; and the weight of the *missorium* is inscribed on the underside in Greek. Silver dishes of this type—this is a particular showpiece—were made for ceremonial occasions. In the scene, the enthroned Emperor is presiding over the appointment of some official and hands over to him the diptych with the Theodosian Code on it.

This silver box for relics was found in Henchir Zirara, Numidia (now the eastern part of Algeria), and it has clear likenesses to certain reliquaries in Italian church treasuries. We cannot say much about their place of origin. However, in both form and feature, this one is wholly in the tradition of European Early Christian art and has close resemblances with other pieces created for the imperial palace. On the lid is portrayed a youthful martyr carrying a garland, while from Heaven a hand bestows the martyr's wreath upon him: this reminds us of carvings at the imperial court of divine bestowal—by the *dextera Domini*—of a victor's laurels on the Emperor. Torches flame on either side of the martyr, a detail often encountered in sepulchral art. Christian symbolic motifs decorate the sides of the reliquary in a continuous band. The waters of Paradise are seen to flow from a mountain on which the Constantinian monogram of Christ appears. A stag and a doe come to drink, and a flock of lambs, with the Lamb of God, also approaches the waters of life. These scenes are located either in Paradise or in the basilica signifying the Church on Earth.

The ship with Christ as helmsman is another symbol representing the Church of Christ. The inscription on this bronze lamp, found near the church of San Stefano Rotondo in Rome, begins with the words: DOMINUS LEGEM DAT ... ("God gives the law ..."), which is another way of saying, "Christ the Master is at the helm"; while the *orant* in the prow must represent the man referred to in the second part of the inscription ... VALERIO SEVERIO EUTRO. VIVAS. Bronze objects from Early Christian times are few and far between, although there are some lamps, figurative weights, and pilgrims' commemorative tokens. They are not easy to classify, since they have stylistic peculiarities which set them well apart from other productions of Early Christian art.

Lamp in the form of a ship. Bronze, height 9⅞″. Fourth–fifth centuries. Museo Archeologico, Florence

◀ *Capsella Africana.* Reliquary. Silver. Fifth century. Museo Sacro, Vatican

Iesus CHristus THeu Yios Soter ("Jesus Christ, Son of God and Redeemer") = ICHTHYS (also the Greek word for "fish"): this was the symbol familiar to all Christians and a token of their avowal of faith. Fish and bread were also symbols of the common meal (the *agape*), of the Eucharist (sacrament of the Lord's Supper), and of belief in salvation through God in the Resurrection. The fish, an ancient Egyptian token of belief in resurrection, now takes on a new Christian significance. The fish symbol is found on catacomb walls as well as in the form of small lockets, of an amulet or talisman nature, worn both as a safeguard and as a secret sign.

Small fish. Bone, length 1⅝″. Early fifth century. Cabinet des Médailles, Paris

As Christianity succeeded in emerging from the catacombs into the open and becoming the official religion, it took over from existing architecture the basic idea of the basilica. The vault of the apse became the place for the presentation of the new religion's claims to offer not only salvation but also revelation, and not least, its claims to historical validity. Here we are confronted by the first powerful symbols of evolving Christianity. Unfortunately, in westward-looking Rome only very few of these early mosaic-decorated apses have survived. One of the earliest—and one considerably altered later—is the apse in the church of Santa Pudenziana in Rome. The mosaic of the vault is very much in the tradition of the Roman pre-Christian art. Its subject matter, so often used in Early Christian art, is Christ among the Apostles. In this case, there is a slight extension of the familiar theme, a reference to the establishment of the Christian Church in Rome. Standing behind the Apostles are personifications of the "two churches," the Jewish-Christian and the Gentile-Christian, described by theologians of the time as *ecclesia ex circumcisione* and *ecclesia ex gentibus* respectively. The place in which all the figures are assembled has the characteristics of the open basilica commonly used in Rome for all kinds of gatherings connected with public affairs. In the background, buildings of an

Christ and the Apostles. Fresco. Fourth century. *Arcosolium* (tomb niche) near crypt of Ampliatus, Catacomb of Domitilla, Rome

Christ and the Twelve Apostles. Mosaic. End of fourth century. Apse of Santa Pudenziana, Rome

imaginary city may be glimpsed; this was the usual way of depicting the Heavenly Jerusalem. It is also possible to see the place in which they are assembled as an open *exedra* such as might be used for a debate by a philosopher and his pupils. But no convincing evidence has been brought forward to prove that the background buildings actually represent the earthly Jerusalem. The cross in the vault of the apse cannot possibly be taken to represent the Cross on Golgotha, for this place of assembly is idealized, imaginary, and the cross is just a symbol. The two female figures are there to represent the two churches, not to represent women who were followers of Christ. This cannot be a New Testament episode but must be a representation of the existing state of the Church of Christ. Such an interpretation is supported by a conventional form of picture which evolved slowly from representations of the Last Supper, and became canonically established, emerging at exactly the same time as the Church. Most of the heads, and the outermost figures, have been renewed in the course of later restorations. The inscription of Pope Innocent I (401–17) is over the mosaic, but it was in fact commissioned by Pope Siricius (384–99).

In the church of Saints Cosmas and Damian, Christ comes striding forth on the clouds and stands between the two chief Apostles, Peter and Paul, who lead the founders of the Church into His presence. Christ is no longer the Lord of this world, no longer just the foremost among the philosophers. He is also Lord of that other world from which He will come to judge the quick and the dead; He reveals Himself here to the Christian community.

In Early Christian art, the apse was the chosen place for the major pictorial statements on great themes. To the paintings and mosaics of the nave believers looked for instruction and example, and there they found Old and New Testament scenes arranged side by side and one above another in areas separated only by a simple horizontal or vertical band of decorative motifs. The illuminators of manuscripts and the catacomb wall painters had prepared the way for this art. When Pope Sixtus had the basilica of Santa Maria Maggiore built between 432 and 440 he could refer to a whole host of prototypes as inspiration for the Biblical scenes of the nave and aisles.

Joshua's Host Before the Walls of Jericho. Nave mosaic. c. 432–40. Santa Maria Maggiore, Rome

It is probably on account of the mosaics of Santa Maria Maggiore that, in spite of one rebuilding after another, the basic features of this important structure are still recognizable. The church stands on the site of an earlier pagan basilica. It was begun in 352 and then under Sixtus III (432–40) entirely rebuilt and richly adorned with mosaics. It has two aisles flanking an exceptionally wide nave with rows of Ionic columns directly supporting an entablature. Rising above the entablature the upper pilastered walls are pierced by arched windows. The present transept and the apse are part of a thirteenth-century rebuilding. The taking over of the ancient basilican form led in the great Roman churches to a spacious plan in which the broad nave is so stressed in contrast to the side aisles that they play hardly any part in the final effect of the building. In this case, the old basilican appearance is even more pronounced, since the placing of the pillars and entablature follows that of the original secular building.

Santa Maria Maggiore, Rome. View of the nave. 352–66, rebuilt 432–40

Santa Sabina on the Aventine, Rome. 425–40

In about 425, the Presbyter Peter of Illyria began the building of Santa Sabina on the Aventine. The building survives in almost its entirety and gives us a good idea of an Early Christian church of the more highly developed type in Rome, uncluttered by misleading additions. The information in the *Liber Pontificalis,* according to which the building was completed under Sixtus III (432–40), describes a whole complex of buildings for the ritual and worship of a large parish. A baptistery was also explicitly mentioned. We can still recognize in the uncompromisingly plain expanse of exterior wall the earlier secular model. At clerestory level, great windows with a network of mullions and transoms ensure that light streams into the nave, the luminous and generous spaces of which are clear evidence of the influence of the architecture of late Antiquity and the earliest years of Christianity. The only comparable example, equally well preserved, is a secular building of late Antiquity, Constantine's basilica in Trier.

Santa Sabina, Rome. Nave and apse. 425–40

Conscientious restorations have preserved for us fully the spacious lines of the church interior. Arcades borne on fluted columns support the upper walls of the nave, with their great window openings, and run all the way to the apse which is as wide as the nave itself. The apse too has three huge windows. Most of the mosaic decoration has gone, but enough of the marble facing remains above the arcades to give an idea of the original richness of the interior. In this marble, which imitates wall construction, are set above each column emblems of Christ Triumphant. In the course of the most recent restorations the open rafters were replaced by a coffered roof, since there was reason to believe that this would be more in keeping with the original. The *schola cantorum,* a kind of fenced-off precinct in front of the chancel, is a later addition, but it must correspond to something similar at the time of the original building.

The superb wooden door is the same age as the church, according to scholarly opinion. Of the twenty-eight carved scenes which used to adorn it, eighteen still remain. The molding with vine branches framing the square and oblong panels is not original work. The subjects are from the Old and New Testaments and their choice suggests an accepted typological series, since each New Testament episode is closely associated with one or more Old Testament episodes of similar import. The linking of the episodes is based on the belief that the "two Testaments do speak with one voice" (*concordia veteris et novi testamenti*).

Baptistery, 432–40. San Giovanni in Fonte, Rome

In addition to the imposing basilican churches, smaller circular or octagonal ones were being built as early as the reign of Constantine, mainly as baptisteries. Several buildings of this kind are known to us as sepulchers. The Constantinian examples were usually of circular or rotunda plan, for instance Santa Costanza in Rome. The Lateran baptistery, San Giovanni in Fonte, was originally a simple, almost circular, building. Of the first structure nothing remains apart from fragments of the encircling walls. In common with other Early Christian buildings, the baptistery of San Giovanni in Fonte was erected over the remains of some Roman baths. Sixtus III (432–40) had the baptistery completely reconstructed according to the accepted form of his time, i.e., on an octagonal ground plan reflecting the shape of the font which was also likely to be octagonal at that time. In San Giovanni in Fonte, however, there is a round font surmounted by a two-storied octagonal colonnade, which shape also dictated the outer contours of the building. In front of the building there is an atrium, with two semicircular exedrae, in exactly the same form as in Santa Costanza. For this reason it has sometimes been assumed that the latter was also originally a baptistery.

San Stefano Rotondo, Rome. 468–83.
Right: exterior. Below: interior

Baptistery. Early fifth
century. Fréjus (Var),
France

The conventions behind these octagonal and circular buildings undoubtedly came from the Eastern Empire, and the outstanding examples are certainly the two memorial churches of Constantine's reign in the Holy Land: the Church of the Nativity and that of the Holy Sepulcher.

San Stefano Rotondo, Rome (page 83), is said to have been modeled on the Church of the Holy Sepulcher in Jerusalem. The circular building of the time of Pope Simplicius (468–83) is now being carefully restored. The conclusions of those who have been studying the building in connection with this work have not

yet been published. In the meantime, we can say merely that the structure is not as well preserved as could be wished. But the main features are still there: the great circular interior colonnade, the architrave set directly on the columns, and the exceptionally wide drum above. These are in their original form. Radical change has been effected by subsequent reconstruction: the arcade in the ambulatory has been walled in so that only the inner ambulatory is intact. The exterior one to which the arcade gave access, and which still has its original outer wall, can still be glimpsed from the ancient apse which has survived. The regular spacing of the columns in the arcade is interrupted by wider spaces at intervals so arranged as to introduce a cruciform accent into what was basically a pagan architectural plan—that of a round building—and which was perhaps incorporated into the Holy Sepulcher church first. Both of the great columns in the middle of the rotunda were inserted at the time of Pope Hadrian I in the eighth century to give more support to the roof over the wide central space.

In Italy, the two imperial towns of Milan and Ravenna were important centers of Christian culture in addition to Rome itself. In the fourth century (c. 385), the great *martyrium* of Sant'Ambrogio was built, and shortly afterward, the octagonal church of San Lorenzo which could also be one of the long series of *martyria* erected in Milan. It may be assumed that the original plan goes back to before the time of Ambrose, the great Latin Father and saint. Some scholars believe that it could have been established under Constantius II. The well-preserved core shows it to be a *tetraconch* with a high central dome—a pattern known to have been favored in the East for *martyria*. However, no martyr's tomb has been proved to have existed at San Lorenzo. A whole group of smaller, centrally planned buildings adjoins the church, the most important of them being the Arian baptistery of Sant'Aquilino lying to the south (left in the picture). Like other early Milan churches, Sant'Aquilino still has remains of the original mosaics which show a great flowering of art in Milan in Saint Ambrose's day and just after, mosaics which cannot have been far behind those of Galla Placidia's mausoleum in Ravenna in quality.

In southern Gaul, the building of Christian edifices spread rapidly from the beginning of the fourth century onward. Most of the basilicas have crumbled away but round buildings and baptisteries are still to be seen. The important baptistery in Marseilles had eight columns surrounding the font and an ambulatory of corresponding size. In Riez, France, the eight columns are connected by small arches to the outer wall and so lead the eye from the cubic shape, lower down, up to the octagon of the dome. In Fréjus, the octagonal font, or piscina, in the middle of the baptistery was placed under a *ciborium,* or freestanding canopy (page 84). The eight main supporting columns now stand directly in front of the wall. The sides of the octagon open into recesses, alternately semicircular and rectangular, and an arcaded clerestory below the dome connects the inner octagonal with the outer square shape.

JUSTINIAN AND RAVENNA

After the removal of the Western Imperial court to the Adriatic naval base of Ravenna, this major city began to win its reputation as one of the greatest art centers of the West, and later of Byzantium. Aquileia, Grado, Trieste, and Parenzo (now Poreč, Yugoslavia) were equally involved in prolific creative efforts, but little of the work of these early years remains in them. In Ravenna, there are still vestiges of the original five-aisled basilica erected about the year 400. The Arian Bishop Neon built the domed octagonal Baptistery of the Orthodox in about 458. It was at one time closely connected with a now vanished cathedral. The large font, traditionally octagonal, was essential for the Early Christian baptismal rite of total immersion. It also dictated the ground plan of the building. A notable feature on the outer walls is the joining of the niches to the octagon by apsidal vaults.

Baptistery of the Orthodox (San Giovanni in Fonte), Ravenna. c. 458

Baptistery of the Orthodox (San Giovanni in Fonte), Ravenna. Interior. c. 458

Baptism of Christ. Dome mosaic. c. 458. Baptistery
of the Orthodox (San Giovanni in Fonte), Ravenna

Mausoleum of Galla Placidia, Ravenna. c. 425 ▶

Directly above the font, in the center of the dome, the mosaic shows the baptism of Christ in the Jordan—a picture of how baptism in the font below is performed. The broad area around it shows a procession of martyrs. The wreaths they carry testify to their having passed through the "baptism of blood." In a further band there are other references to salvation in the form of the four books of the Gospels lying open on altars; in panels between these there are thrones, an allusion to the empty throne of the Apocalypse.

The Imperial Palace at Ravenna had its own great palatine chapel, Santa Croce, of which only a few ruins remain. To the vestibule before the nave (the former now vanished, the latter fragmentary) the Chapel of Saint Lawrence, now known as the Mausoleum of Galla Placidia, was joined. Galla Placidia was the wife of Constantius III (co-emperor with Honorius) who died in 421. She had the little mausoleum built in 425 after her return from Constantinople. Having led an adventurous life, she died in Rome and was buried in her chapel, where there are also the tombs of her husband and of a few other relations. The simple building has external walls of skillfully arranged brickwork with blind arches and small window apertures. Both inner and outer ground levels were raised considerably in later ages, so that the original proportions have been much altered. The present building is only 49 feet long by 42$^{1}/_{2}$ feet wide. It constitutes a simple and ideal shrine for the mosaics which, resplendent in the half-light, adorn the interior sumptuously under the star-studded dome with its great Cross (see page 90).

The Cross in a Starry Firmament with Symbols of the Evangelists. Dome mosaic. c. 425. Mausoleum of Galla Placidia, Ravenna

The steeply cambered dome thrusts its pendentives down to frame the areas with representations of the Apostles and martyrs. The dark-blue ground of the mosaics adds to the darkness of the cupola, which admits no direct daylight, so that the golden mosaic pieces of the stars sparkle and gleam all the more. The stars are scattered all round the Cross which is the center of this firmament and the principal symbol in this cruciform building. Symbols of the four Evangelists link the circle of the dome to the square plan of the crossing below.

The lunettes in the recesses, the arms of the cruciform ground plan, complement the other themes represented. In the central niche, Saint Lawrence (deacon of Pope Sixtus II) appears with the gridiron, the symbol of his martyrdom, and the bookcase containing the Gospels of which he, as deacon, had charge. In other recesses we see the symbol of Salvation, in this case a stream from which stags are drinking, as well as the time-honored Christian symbol of the Good Shepherd. The barrel vaults of the recesses, in almost total darkness, are lavishly ornamented.

Mausoleum of Galla Placidia, Ravenna. Interior. c. 425

Sarcophagus, said to be that of Valentinian III, son of Galla Placidia. Fifth century. Marble. Mausoleum of Galla Placidia, Ravenna

The Lamb of God by "streams of living water," approached by two other lambs, is a much simplified image of the power of Christianity to succor and save, so often represented in Early Christian churches. This symbolic scene appears on a tomb, said to be that of her son Valentinian III, in the Mausoleum of Galla Placidia.

In the year 493 Theodoric, the Ostrogothic king, gained possession of Ravenna and later had a two-storied domed building erected there as his mausoleum. As was usual in the tombs of heroes and martyrs in late Antiquity, the lower chamber contained the sarcophagus and the upper one was intended as a meeting place for the cult of the dead person. The dome, made from one huge ashlar block, has twelve projecting corbels with the names of the twelve Apostles, signifying that this king of the Ostrogoths regarded himself, just as the Emperors of Byzantium did, as Christ's successor in the world and had his own entourage of twelve friends or counselors. His great example, Constantine the Great, had surrounded himself in his own mausoleum with twelve monumental piers inscribed with the names of the Apostles. The Germanic conqueror adapted himself to the art and culture of the conquered country. With the taking of the city by the Byzantine general Belisarius (540), the Ostrogothic overlordship in Ravenna came to an end and Theodoric's monument was never completed.

Mausoleum of Theodoric the Great, Ravenna. c. 526

San Giovanni Evangelista, Ravenna. c. 425. Above: exterior. Right: view toward choir

Galla Placidia, daughter of Theodosius and half sister of Honorius and Arcadius, was the founder of one of the oldest ecclesiastical buildings in Ravenna. Because of her disagreements with Honorius, she was for some time confined to the Eastern Imperial court; after the death of her hostile brother she went back to Ravenna. On her journey she made a solemn vow, while a tempest raged over the seas, to build a church in honor of Saint John the Evangelist (San Giovanni Evangelista). The chronicler Agnellus gives the text of the dedicatory inscription: "To the saintly and supremely blessed John the Evangelist, Galla Placidia Augusta and her son, Placidus Valentinianus Augustus, and her daughter, Justa Grata Honoria Augusta, fulfill the vow made for delivery from peril on the seas." This inscription is now lost. The church immediately adjoins the site of the imperial palace in the *regio Caesarum* ("district of the Caesars") and there is evidence that a former hall of the palace may have been absorbed into the original structure. The many vicissitudes through which it has passed make it difficult for us to envisage its original state; the nave and chancel shown on the facing page are fairly close to the original plan, based on a nave with two aisles, the nave rising to a considerable height and terminating in a comparatively shallow apse with an extensive triumphal arch. On either side of the apse, at the ends of the aisles, there is a chamber; these are the *prothesis* and the *diaconicon,* both important in the early cult. At the back of the polygonal apse, three arched windows, now walled in, are surmounted by a most unusual row of arched openings, more numerous than—but in the same proportions as—the three windows below. Whether this arcade is a later addition, making a considerable difference to the general appearance of the interior, or whether it was part of Galla Placidia's original building—a feature imitating the rich variety of window arrangements found in early Byzantine palaces—is still an open question despite much research and many theories. The descriptions of the first mosaic decorations in the *Liber Pontificalis Ecclesiae Ravennatis* ("Episcopal Book of the Church in Ravenna") of the ninth century, and elsewhere, do not help us. We learn from them, however, that the apse and the triumphal arch were covered with mosaics. In the middle of the apse, Christ was enthroned with the twelve sealed books of the Apostles around Him. Below was the now vanished votive inscription. Saint John was represented on the triumphal arch above with, on either side of him, the deliverance from the tempest at sea, a scene we know from a pair of miniatures from the fourteenth century. Beside the representation of Christ, and below it, there were three other decorated areas in the apse. One showed the Evangelists; one Saint Peter Chrysologus, archbishop of Ravenna, celebrating mass between members of the imperial house of Theodosius; and one contained *intarsia* work (mosaic of wooden pieces). The siting of these three zones is more easily imagined if we assume the arcaded windows to have been an original feature, though in that case the area left for the representation of Christ was certainly very small.

MAXIMIAN

◄ *Justinian and His Suite*. Mosaic. Consecrated by
Archbishop Maximian in 547. San Vitale, Ravenna

San Vitale, Ravenna. Consecrated 547

The art of Ravenna under Byzantine sway came to its full flowering with the accession of the Eastern Roman Emperor Justinian and during the years that followed. His representatives in Ravenna were the archbishops Victor (538–45) and Maximian (546–56), the latter figuring everlastingly in the history of art for the ivory throne he had made (see page 101). They erected the church of San Vitale, which Maximian consecrated in 547, with the help of a financial magnate named Julianus Argentarius. Shortly before the ceremony, the dedicatory mosaic showing Justinian, in which the name of Maximian was expressly mentioned, was put in place. Opposite Justinian, his wife Theodora with her royal household is shown.

The church is seen from behind the apse, with the apse on the right of the illustration. The small round building belongs to the *presbytery* (precinct for the officiating clergy between altar and choir). The main entrance, with transverse narthex, lies on the far side. Both ground plan and superstructure have Byzantine antecedents in the buildings raised by Justinian in Constantinople at about the same time. San Vitale is the only surviving octagonal church of truly Byzantine character to be found in the West.

97

As was the case with Galla Placidia's little mausoleum, San Vitale combines a sumptuous interior with a comparatively stark exterior. In a subtle sequence of forms, the octagonal ground plan merges, through the roundheaded arches of the central portion of the building, into the circular shape of the dome. The surviving mosaics are mainly in the presbytery and the apse. Much of the wall space was covered with a marble facing, much of which is still in place, but the gilding on the capitals, which was vital to the play of light upon the details, has faded away. In the apse, Christ is represented, standing on the globe of the world, with the patron saint of this church, Saint Vitalis.

The presbytery has, near the Evangelists and the dedicatory scenes, a series of Old Testament scenes on the theme of the sacrament of the Mass: Melchizedek's sacrifice and the offering up of Isaac are contrasted with the bloodless sacrifice of Christ in the Mass. There are also some events from the life of Moses.

Throne of Archbishop Maximian (546–56). Ivory, 59 x 23⁵/₈". Archiepiscopal Museum, Ravenna

Melchizedek's Sacrifice. Mosaic on south wall of presbytery. c. 547. San Vitale, Ravenna

The presbytery gallery devotes a splendid array of costly materials to theological interpretations of the various stages of the Mass which plainly relate to the location of the altar in this spot. The exquisite pierced decoration on the capitals, all handwork of filigree delicacy, is in the Byzantine tradition and points to the collaboration of Byzantine workers.

The throne of Maximian is shown by an inscription to have been the ivory throne of the archbishop of Ravenna who consecrated the church. The panels were either fashioned in Constantinople itself or in Ravenna under the influence of Byzantine artists: we have no convincing evidence to settle this point (see also pages 126 f.).

In the seaport of old Ravenna (today a flat arable plain) is Sant'Apollinare in Classe, Ravenna's most remarkable basilica—a type of building that was being continued along with the domed, centrally planned structures. The church was consecrated at the same time as San Vitale and financed by the same Julianus Argentarius. Like its namesake, Sant'Apollinare Nuovo, it has three aisles and a raised presbytery. The uncomplicated exterior is reminiscent of a Roman basilica. Capitals and columns were probably imported from Byzantium, and there is a Syrian flavor to the architectural treatment of the buildings around the apse. The masterly handling of the masons' work is very much a Byzantine skill. The towers alongside both the Apollinaris churches (Saint Apollinaris was Ravenna's first bishop and patron saint) have been shown by recent investigations to be medieval additions.

Here again, we see the emphasis on the presbytery with its handsome mosaic adornment. Indeed, the apse mosaics are the only ones that date from the foundation of the building. The patron saint appears here with twelve lambs as shepherd of his church, and just as Christ does on the triumphal arch as Shepherd of His Apostles and of Christendom. Above, in the summit of the apse, is the Cross of Christ between Moses and Elijah. Such a composition indicates the Transfiguration as the theme of the apse. The jeweled cross is symbolic of the immediate presence of the Transfigured Christ. In Early Christian art, a symbol is to be equated with what it represents, for form and content are still one; for instance, the Cross in the starry sky in the cosmic sphere is not only the symbol of the Transfigured Christ but also Christ Himself.

Sant'Apollinare in Classe, Ravenna. Consecrated 549   Apse of Sant'Apollinare in Classe, Ravenna ▶

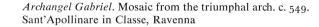

Archangel Gabriel. Mosaic from the triumphal arch. c. 549. Sant'Apollinare in Classe, Ravenna

The triumphal arch invariably has a Christological theme on it. In this case it is Christ Himself with His lambs and symbols of the Evangelists. The two sides of the entrance to the sanctuary have mosaics of the Archangels Gabriel and Michael. The inclusion of Constantine IV Pogonatus (668–85) in a donor scene permits the dating of this particular mosaic to about 675.

The church of Sant'Apollinare Nuovo is architecturally similar to Sant'Apollinare in Classe. It was not given its name until it came to enshrine the saint's relics in the ninth century. It was built as a palatine church under Theodoric the Great and it was at this time that the first mosaics were made. Later the church was taken over for the Orthodox cult and renamed Sancti Martini in Coelo Aureo. Then, all parts of the mosaic which seemed to support Arian doctrine, and all allusions to Theodoric, had to be removed. The mosaics of the nave complement those of the apse in Sant'Apollinare in Classe, giving us a good idea of what a complete Ravenna basilica must have been like. From the west wall, with its mosaics depicting Theodoric's palace and the port of Classis, two long processions of martyrs wend their way along either side of the nave, one toward Christ Enthroned and the other toward the enthroned Virgin and the Magi worshiping in her presence. Between the windows above are patriarchs and prophets, and, over their heads, New Testament episodes.

Procession of Female Martyrs. Nave mosaic. Begun c. 504 but with later alterations. Sant'Apollinare
Nuovo, Ravenna

While the New Testament scenes and standing figures between the windows were unlikely to raise political problems or to offend the Orthodox, the mosaics lower down the nave walls had to be fundamentally altered, when the Orthodox cult took over, to a strictly Byzantine iconographical program. The mosaics of Theodoric's palace and of the port of Classis which appeared in the church were obviously colored by political notions alien to the new rulers and were far too worldly, so the Byzantine bishop Agnellus had the whole group worked over to bring it into conformity. He had the figures standing in the arcades of the palace removed and the gaps filled with curtains, their folds secured in a knot. The mosaic of the worshiping Magi was reworked yet again in later times.

Adoration of the Magi. Nave mosaic. c. 560. Sant'Apollinare Nuovo, Ravenna

If we compare the mosaic of the Magi with that of the deacon in the Baptistery of the Orthodox, we can see clearly that a span of a hundred years separates them. The Byzantines had discovered and perfected their own independent forms in Constantinople during this time, and they now imported them as occupiers into this Italian province.

The Golden Gate, Constantinople (Istanbul). Wall with propylaea-like gateway. c. 447; gate c. 390

JUSTINIAN AND BYZANTIUM

Until the early years of the sixth century, Constantinople clearly modeled herself on the Western Imperial capital city of Rome, trying to capture the essence of Rome for the East. The layout, with its fortified surrounding walls, its imperial forums, its palaces and temples, had the essential features of the ideal city. But as early as the opening years of the fifth century the eastern capital was the focus, for the whole Mediterranean region, of developments in the art and science of architecture. It was now her turn to embark upon building projects. When Alaric was attacking Rome and the chaos of the years of the mass migrations brought official building in Rome to a standstill, Theodosius II completed the defenses of Constantinople. Between 410 and 420 the towering landward walls went up, with close on two hundred fortified towers built with a sophisticated and very decorative technique of bricks alternating with ashlar, a bulwark against overland attack which was complemented on the seaward side with another wall about three hundred and fifty feet long. Its domed towers, with rooms supported on arches, are masterpieces of Byzantine round building. Instead of the principal street or "way" dear to the Romans, Constantinople had a wide processional route lined with churches and cloisters. The Golden Gate, too, played its part in imperial processions. It was here that the Emperor came into the city after his coronation.

The building shown on the facing page was begun early in the fourth century by the Emperor Galerius (305–11) as an addition to his triumphal arch in Salonika. Theodosius I then had it rebuilt as a church, transforming the simple rotunda with its barrel-vaulted niches, by providing it with an apse and an ambulatory. This is an example of the logical alteration of a pagan burial monument into a building for Christian rites.

Saint George, Salonika. Original building 306–11, rebuilt by Theodosius I as a palatine chapel c. 390

Round or small cruciform buildings were originally reserved in Constantinople for sepulchral and baptismal uses. To begin with, the more important churches were always of a purely basilican type in the Mediterranean classical tradition and followed Roman prototypes fairly closely.

Only the proportions, the broad central nave, the huge octagonal apse, the rows of columns supporting architraves, together with the broad narthex in front of it are purely Byzantine peculiarities of the church erected by the patrician Studios to replace an earlier building. The alternation of brick with layers of ashlar is a typically Byzantine technique, and it was used on a considerable scale in the building of the great land walls. The same general scheme, with a wide, short nave, was to be used for the principal church of Byzantium, Hagia Sophia.

When Justinian had suppressed the Nika insurrection in 532, he set about the rebuilding of his capital, Constantinople, making good the destruction brought about by such vehement strife and taking the opportunity to introduce radical changes. For his more important churches he relied almost entirely on the plan prevail-

Monastery church of Saint John Studios, Constantinople (Istanbul). c. 463

Hagia Sophia, Constantinople (Istanbul). Consecrated 537

ing in the Syrian eastern areas, that of the cross-shaped, domed church; from this time onward it was, in many variations, to prevail over all other forms in Byzantium. The adoption of this Syrian model marks a decisive break with Western tradition. We should not be misled here into supposing that the two builders employed by Justinian, Anthemius of Tralles and Isidorus of Miletus, had a comprehensive classical education at their disposal. The architects to whom he entrusted his great Hagia Sophia came from Asia Minor, from Anatolia, where the domed building predominated. Both were mathematicians and as such highly thought of in their day. They were able to introduce greater flexibility into the vault, a new freedom which left its mark on all subsequent Byzantine architecture. They met superbly all of Justinian's requirements, not only for sheer magnitude, but also for architectural beauty and unprecedented technical perfection. This was their answer to his demand for "the raising of an edifice which has never been equaled since the time of Adam and never will be equaled."

Their outstanding feat was to lead the thrust of the colossal central dome down into the adjoining zones of the building so harmoniously and so imperceptibly that they integrated every part of the church into a unity within which each area fulfilled its function while contributing to the general harmony and rhythm.

Hagia Sophia. View into the dome. Consecrated 537, dome rebuilt 562

Procopius (*De Aedificiis*), historian of the life and times of Justinian, writes of this dome in these terms: "It does not appear to rest on a solid building, but rather to hang from the heavens as though on a golden chain, a tent poised over the space below." He tells us that the entire structure was clothed in mosaics. San Vitale in Ravenna can perhaps give us some idea of its appearance.

◀ Hagia Sophia. Interior. Consecrated 537

Capital of gallery column. Marble. c. 530. Hagia Sophia ▶

The church of Saints Sergius and Bacchus (both very early fourth-century martyrs) was commissioned at the same period by Justinian and his wife Theodora. It represents a different interpretation of the octagonal core plan, the one used also for Justinian's San Vitale in Ravenna. The central area is an octagon placed out of alignment with the irregular square shape formed by the outer walls of the church. Through the octagon's outward openings, divided by pairs of columns on two stories, the walls of the encircling ambulatory appear from the inside as an enveloping shell. In contrast with San Vitale, only four sides of the octagon curve outward in apselike alcoves, lending it the overall impression of an approximately square shape. The round church with ambulatories enclosing an octagon, the form of the Early Christian mausoleum and baptistery, has been converted here into a spatial unity. Perhaps it is this development which is the most decisive contribution of Justinian architecture (that is to say, the new manner of linking core, galleries, and ambulatory). In place of the alignment of the outer walls with the octagon, there now enters into the picture a feeling for a freer arrangement of the space, all parts of the building being united under, and all spatial relationships controlled by, the dome. Saints Sergius and Bacchus, Hagia Sophia, and Ravenna's San Vitale are the three finest examples of the new architectural approach.

Saints Sergius and Bacchus, Constantinople (Istanbul). 527–36. Left: exterior. Right: interior

The Church of Saint Irene, begun as a basilica under Constantine, was also destroyed by the Nika rioters. The building as we have it today is typical of a Justinian domed church, yet in its present form it still has strong affinities with the basilica and with the domed buildings of Asia Minor.

The new building was undertaken at the same time as the rebuilding of Hagia Sophia in 532. With both churches there was to be inevitable disaster through the overhasty use of techniques for building the domes. The choir side was not sufficiently solid to take the thrust of its dome, more than fifty feet in diameter, and fell in under the weight. After this mishap, the church was remodeled with a more elongated ground plan allowing for a succession of interrelated areas with walls and pierced screens of rich workmanship, all arranged to stress the church's longitudinal axis. After a fire in the year 564, the church once again needed to be rebuilt. In 740 an earthquake destroyed it yet again. The present building is the one erected after the earthquake. Since this was not a period of any startling innovations, we can assume that the combination of two domes and a three-aisled basilica, with the technique of mounting the domes on drums above wide barrel-vaulted side recesses, is the same as the one that had survived until then from the sixth century. Above the side aisles and the narthex are galleries; the result is that the aisles seem to be little more than supporting walls, with great scooped-out arches, for the domes. From this, the building draws its effect of massiveness and its various elements their appearance of having been wrought out of the wall itself, although standing independently of one another. The main dome, itself covering a small gallery, is but one element in a unity.

Saint Irene, Istanbul (Constantinople). Begun 532, rebuilt 740. Left: exterior. Below: interior

Saint Demetrius, Salonika. First structure, fifth century; almost entirely reconstructed after the fire of 1917

In places untouched by the hand of Justinian and unaffected by his reforming zeal, some basilicas of the old pattern survived. Even after destruction by fire in later years they were rebuilt in the same fashion.

In the years 412 and 413 Saint Demetrius in Salonika was founded by Leontius, Prefect of Illyria, as a sepulchral monument to the great and deeply revered martyr Demetrius, but the building which was completed in the course of the fifth century was devoured by flames in 630. It was at once rebuilt and covered inside with splendid mosaics. Again in 1917 it was burned to the ground, but in our own times it has risen once more, still in its old style.

This church represents the purest form of the five-aisled basilica with cross transept in the Eastern Empire. The lofty nave, terminating in an apse, two-storied throughout its length, has the look of a broad, well-lit highway to the chancel. The arcades on the upper level open laterally into the galleries over the aisles adjoining the nave. Beyond them there are, either side, two more aisles that do not, however, have galleries. The arcades on either side of the nave are divided into three great zones by the use, every four columns, of a large square pier.

The church was conceived as a monument for the saint and his tomb lies in front of the apse. It is the focal point of a rectangular area, jutting out either side of the church in transepts, which can be seen very distinctly from the outside as an oblong extension rising to the height of the inner aisles. The intersection of the nave with a transverse area before the apse is architecturally sophisticated and creates an unusual setting for the tomb of the martyr. The same structural characteristics are found at Rome in San Paolo Fuori le Mura and in Egypt in the basilica of Saint Menas. They are plainly Christian innovations related to certain aspects of ritual. Basilicas with transepts have influenced Western architecture even more than the centrally planned domed buildings of Byzantium which were restricted almost entirely to the East.

Saint Demetrius, Salonika. Interior after rebuilding

Now that Christianity had become the official religion of the Empire, it was time for it to adapt itself to meeting the state's need to have its authority and sovereignty publicly exhibited. In the ceremonial of the Byzantine imperial court, which in Constantine's time had simply become the ceremonial of the Christian religion as well, art was called upon to minister to the claims to power and the demands for luxury of powerful court circles, which had, particularly in Justinian's time, raised their expectations to a very high level.

Ivory, which had been highly esteemed in earlier centuries for its rarity and costliness, was now also acknowledged to have certain imperial qualities. Pieces of furniture for ceremonial use were decorated with it, and for official gifts from imperial and consular donors this material was often preferred to all others. The ivory said to represent the Empress Ariadne, probably dating from about 500, is a good example of the way in which the imperial family chose to be depicted. The Empress wears her robes of state with crown, scepter, and imperial orb surmounted by a cross. She stands under a baldachin or canopy supported on fluted pillars and understood as a sign of majesty. The style and relief treatment indicate Eastern origin.

Empress Ariadne. Ivory diptych, $11^7/_8 \times 3^7/_8''$. c. 500. Museo Nazionale del Bargello, Florence

The diptych with a portrait of an unknown poet or scholar, perhaps Ausonius, Boethius, or even Seneca, looks back to an earlier tradition for both form and content and is in direct line of descent from the classical revival initiated by Theodosius. The mannered handling of the folds of the garments is nevertheless likely to be proof of Eastern influence and links this piece with Egyptian work of the same era.

Poet and Muse. Ivory diptych, each leaf 13³/₈ x 5″. c. 500. Cathedral, Monza

Barberini Ivory. Imperial diptych. Ivory, $13^3/_8$ x $10^1/_2$". c. 500. From the Barberini Collection, Rome. The Louvre, Paris

In the year 500 or thereabouts, this five-panel ivory, named after a former owner, was made and bestowed as a gift, no doubt by one of the Emperors. With the two-part consular diptychs in mind, it has been styled an "imperial diptych," although it comprises only a single leaf. The personage represented is probably the Emperor Anastasius, who ruled in Byzantium from 491 to 518. On the reverse of this ivory tablet there is a list of the bishops of Trier up to 675, so we may assume that the recipient of this gift officiated in the western part of the Empire.

The *Barberini Ivory* shows the Emperor's return from a victorious campaign, for which a special celebration was provided in Byzantine court ceremonial. *Terra* (earth), beneath the horse, clasps his foot in an attitude of submission. A Scythian warrior puts his hand on the lance in token of defeat. A *nike* hovers, preparing to crown the victor. Christ appears above the Emperor, His scepter, the Cross, in His hand, in a round shield supported by two angels. To one side stands one of the victorious generals as an attendant figure, while in the bottom panel the peoples of the world pay homage to their Emperor who has conquered in Christ's name. We can accept that this is an exact representation of the ceremonial carried out by a victorious Emperor in the processional parade and described as an *adventus*.

Angels could also be represented on diptychs (right) as rulers and conquerors in the name of Christ. For Michael, the leader of the heavenly host, such a representation was particularly appropriate. Similarly, angels may well appear on other tablets, also of Byzantine origin, as representatives of Rome and Constantinople, the two imperial cities.

Archangel Michael. One leaf of a diptych. Ivory, 16⁷/₈ x 5⁵/₈". c. 500. British Museum, London

Christ Between Peter and Paul and *Mary Between Archangels*. Ivory diptych, each leaf 11³/₈ x 5¹/₈". Mid-sixth century. State Museums, Berlin

Procession with Relics. Ivory. 5¹/₈ x 10¹/₄″. Sixth or seventh century. Cathedral treasury, Trier

Ivory diptychs with religious themes shown on one side had a practical purpose in the church of their day: on their blank wax-coated side the names of saints, martyrs, or the dead, for whom the believers were asked to intercede, were written. Traditionally the diptych was a two-part writing tablet with its writing surfaces, susceptible to damage, hinged to close upon one another, and ornamental features were confined to the outside surfaces.

Christ between Peter and Paul, and Mary with the Archangels Gabriel and Michael, are shown enthroned in niches like secular rulers with their vassals. The edges of the garments' folds, the flat style as though drawn, and the stiff composition of the groups of figures point in this case to a Byzantine provenance in the mid-sixth century. Traces of an inscribed character on the border are said to show Maximian's monogram, which would relate the Berlin diptych to the throne of Maximian associated with that same bishop of Ravenna.

Despite the thickness of the plaque and the height of the relief, it is fairly obvious from the subject matter that the Trier ivory was originally part of a reliquary. To the right, an empress stands in front of a church still being built; she is in court dress and carries a scepter topped with a cross. In front of the mule-drawn four-wheeled chariot, the usual means of transporting relics, an emperor advances in procession toward the church. Spectators at the palace windows are swinging censers. Research so far, based on the fact that the plaque was found in Trier, has named the emperor and the empress as Constantine and Helena, but there is no general agreement on this. In fact, the personages, the place, and the circumstances of this extraordinarily interesting work are still to be positively identified. The technical level, as well as the hairstyles portrayed, suggest the sixth or early seventh centuries as the earliest possible date. The architectural scheme of the church, however, would not have been applied to a new building in Constantinople at that time. It may well, therefore, be a scene commemorating the founding of a church in Trier by Helena: the cross on her shoulder is an attribute arguing persuasively for the identification of this empress as Constantine's mother.

The separate plaques for the ivory facings of the throne of Archbishop Maximian of Ravenna (546–56) were the work of various artists, all of them probably trained in Byzantium (see page 100). Since Maximian was much in favor with Justinian and Theodora, we can surmise that the Byzantine court either sent him the throne or supplied the artists. The sharp differences in style of the individual plaques on this piece—which we are able to date with a possible error of only ten years, thanks to an inscription—may indicate that there was a workshop in Ravenna with a Byzantine carver in charge. If this were so, we could ascribe the two groups of scenes from the life of Joseph on the sides of the throne, with their skillful arrangement of the figures, to an Italian assistant working under a Byzantine master who would himself have been responsible for the imposing carved portraits of the Apostles on the front. But their kinship with the small carvings of the five-panel *Barberini Diptych* (page 122) indicates more credibly the "revival" movement, initiated by Justinian, with its renewed interest in pagan Antiquity. The peak of achievement during this renaissance was reached by the artists of the *Poet and Muse* diptych and the London *Archangel Michael* already described (see pages 121 and 123).

Facing page: *Two Evangelists*; below: *Joseph Measuring Corn for His Brothers*. Ivory panels from the throne of Archbishop Maximian. Mid-sixth century. Archiepiscopal Museum, Ravenna

Monza Ampullae. Pilgrims' flasks. Embossed silver. Before 600. Cathedral treasury, Monza

The age of Justinian, indeed the whole of the sixth century, produced splendid examples of the gold- and silversmith's art which went back to models in Antiquity. Most of these superb pieces are from finds in Syria, Cyprus, and the Black Sea coasts. The official hallmarks for the years between 490 and 650 give definite indications of the date of manufacture for many of them and point to the existence of an imperial workshop in Byzantium.

Comparison with these works suggests a Byzantine origin for the liturgical vase found at Homs in Syria. The filling of the spaces between the finely worked medallion heads with carefully designed ornaments indicates a metropolitan courtly style which Syrian art imitated but did not equal.

In the sixth century, pilgrims were traveling from the remotest regions in search of the Holy Places in Palestine. At that time there came into being a kind of "souvenir industry" which also had to meet courtly tastes, both temporal and spiritual. This explains such collections of silver bottles as that in the Monza Cathedral treasury, once the property of Theodolinda, a Lombard queen, and probably a gift from Pope Gregory I (590–604), all of which are thus likely to be of the late sixth century. The Monza ampullae were used for carrying the *chrism* (holy oil). Their decoration is based on events in the Scriptures associated with the actual places from which the oils came. They show Christ's sepulcher and the Resurrection, and some show the Ascension. On the flask to the left is the favorite theme, the women at the Tomb. On the right-hand flask, this scene is accompanied by a ring of medallions representing a series of scenes from the life of Christ, ranging from the Annunciation to the Ascension. These silversmiths' pieces are definitely Palestinian in origin and exerted an important influence on the art of the whole Western world. They enabled artists to find out about how themes were presented pictorially in the Holy Land and to use these examples in the decoration of their own churches.

◀ Emesa Vase. Embossed silver, height 17³⁄₈″, diameter 11³⁄₈″. Found near Emesa (Homs). The Louvre, Paris

This ornamental collar with an *encolpion* (Greek term for an ornament to be worn on the breast) comes from a hoard discovered in Egypt. The front of the collar consists of coins; the latest of them shows the Emperor Maurice (Flavius Tiberius Mauricius, 582–602). The middle portrait is surrounded by an inscription, "Lord, assist the wearer." The hanging medallion of the breast ornament, with its fine openwork frame, has the Annunciation scene on the front and the Marriage at Cana on the reverse, thus testifying to belief in Christ as the Son of God and in the sacrament of the Eucharist. In a gold hoard found in Cyprus, there were not only medallions and necklaces of the same date but also a plaque with a medallion portrait of a saint wearing a throat ornament of this type. It bears the official stamp of the time of the Emperor Phocas (602–10).

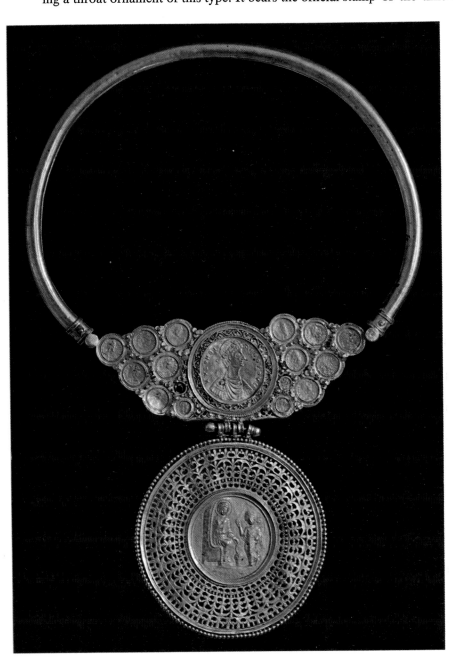

It is extremely difficult to establish the place of origin for silver pieces of about the year 600. The paten found in Riha bears the hallmark of the capital. The characters and content of the text indicate a Syrian origin. The silver hallmarks have here and there been damaged by a silversmith's tools, so it is possible that the piece was made in the capital, assayed and stamped there as a plain silver bowl, then embossed and ornamented in Syria. Another silver bowl (now in the Archaeological Museum, Istanbul) with hallmarks and the same designs on it was found at Stuma in Syria, and this one similarly stands apart from the "Greek renaissance" movement in art. It is a striking fact that the art which in its modes and forms was pre-Christian and pre-Theodosian usually chose nonreligious themes. These can sometimes be a matter of local preference; they can also depend on the range of interests, with an inherited program of subjects for treatment, of given workshops or craftsmen's groups. The conclusion reached by modern scholars from this is that, in Byzantine art, realistic visual images of human beings were permissible but representa-

Communion of the Apostles. Paten. Embossed silver, partially gilded. End of sixth century. Diameter 13³/₄″. Found at Riha, Syria. Dumbarton Oaks Collection, Washington D.C.

◄ Neck and breast ornament of gold coins in a gold setting. c. 600; the latest of the coins was minted before 582. From Egypt. State Museums, Berlin

tions of God and of sacred episodes and scenes had to be a kind of spiritual synthesis of themes rather than a literal rendering. No doubt we have here one of the grounds for the series of events which brought about a break in Byzantine figurative art, after which the hieratic stylistic bias, renouncing figurative representation in the round, was all-pervasive. The strife and tension of iconoclasm in the eighth and ninth centuries resulted in the banning of pictorial and sculptural images of divine beings and sacred scenes. In their place came decorations using animals and fables. The cross alone remained as a spiritual symbol, representing "that which could not be represented."

Several dishes with scenes from the life of David, and all with the hallmark of Heraclius (610–41), were found in Cyprus. The same mark is on one showing a satyr and a maenad which was found in the Black Sea area. Their close similarities in the suggestion of landscape, in the emphasis of the outlines, in the suppleness of the modeling, and not least in the treatment of folds at the extremities of the garments, are such that one is almost tempted to attribute all of them to one workshop. In the two examples on the facing page, the composition in the round and the subject of the first suggest direct borrowing from pagan originals; this also applies to the representation of David overcoming the bear, which is really a reproduction of a sacrifice to Mithras, with an allusion to Christ in the shape of David. For the scene of the marriage of David, reference should be made to the *missorium* of Theodosius I in Madrid (page 71), but there the figures are so closely confined in the space under the arches that a Roman prototype of late Antiquity is more likely than a Greek one. We can be certain that all these pieces are representative of official art under Heraclius, art with a pronounced tendency to use pagan and Christian concepts in very close association and with courtly overtones.

◀ *Marriage of David.* Silver dish, diameter 10⅝″. 610–29. Archaeological Museum, Nicosia

Silenus and Maenad. Silver dish, diameter 10⅛″. 610–29. The Hermitage, Leningrad

David Slaying a Bear. Silver dish. 610–29. Archaeological Museum, Nicosia

Hare Nibbling at a Bunch of Grapes. Wool woven on linen, 8^1/$_2$ x 8″. Sixth century. From Egypt. Private collection

Glass lamp. Sixth century. Cathedral treasury, Saint Mark's, Venice

Contemporary documents and works of art give us an idea of the magnificence of the display at the Byzantine court and of the major contribution made by costly fabrics to all its luxury. As early as the fifth century, there is an account of a senator whose robes of office were adorned with a whole cycle of episodes from the life of Christ. Justinian's Hagia Sophia was enriched with figured hangings which were patterned with more or less the same themes as the mosaics of San Vitale in Ravenna and other places. The vast demand led to the establishment of numerous textile workshops, and these became widespread, principally in Egypt and Syria, most of them under the control of the imperial court. The market for the more expensive silks was so lively that in the sixth century, under Justinian, silkworms were imported from China. The historic details of the silk weaving industry are as difficult to establish as are the sources of individual pieces. As a result of widespread finds in the Nile region, it was thought that large-scale textile production flourished there; then one piece turned out to be most informative: it had an inscription from Heraclea in Thrace. The Vatican silks showing the Annunciation (facing page) and the Nativity were long thought to be of Syrian or Egyptian workmanship. Recently, on stylistic grounds, they have been attributed to the capital itself. Persia furnished not only the silk but also the techniques of silk spinning and weaving. Sassanian motifs, especially in the representation of animals and of battle scenes, are frequently identifiable in the fabrics found in Antinoë. Some pieces, on account of such scenes, have

The Annunciation. Silk twill on red ground, diameter of circle 14¹/₈″. c. 600. Vatican Museums, Rome

been classified as Persian importations. Foreign influences seem in certain respects to have fluctuated in accordance with the fortunes of war. During the Persian Wars of Justinian, Persian influence was strong; at a later date (c. 635) the Arab invasions in the time of Heraclius cut off supplies of Persian manufacture and Islamic influences then predominated in Byzantium.

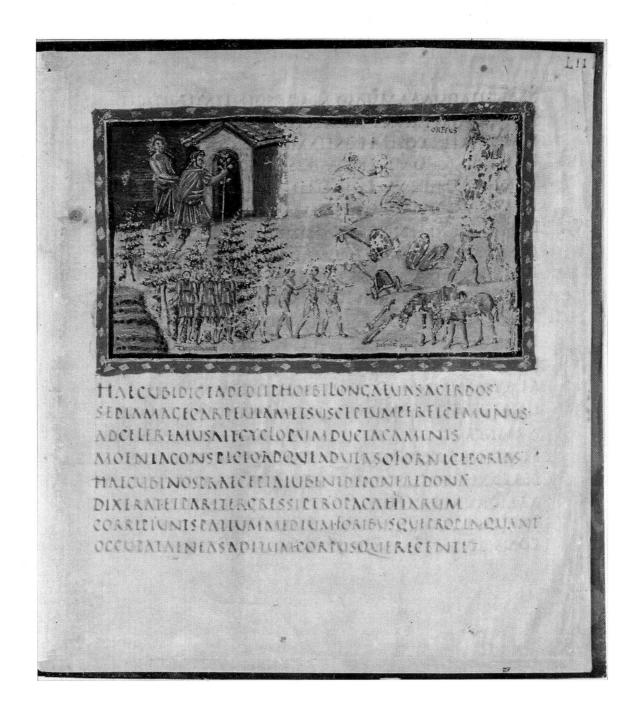

HAECUBIDICTADEDITPHOEBILONCAEUASACERDOS
SEDIAMACECABREUIAMEISUSCEPTUMPERFICEMUNUS
ADCELERIMUSAITCYCLOPUMDUCIACAMINIS
MOENIACONSPICIOADQUIADUITASOLORNICEPORIAS
HAECUBINOSRAICETIAIUBENIDIPONEADONA
DIXERATETPARITERGRESSICEROPACATIARUM
CORRIPIUNTSPATIUMMEDIUMFORIBUSQUIEROLINQUANT
OCCUPATAENEASADITUMCORPUSQUERECENTII

Illustration to Virgil's *Georgics*. Early fifth century. From the *Vatican Virgil,* fol. III recto (?). Cod. lat. 3225, Biblioteca Vaticana, Rome

It was in the sixth century that the representation of Christian themes in book illustration, and thus the new art of the miniature, became established. At first the illustration of ancient texts was limited to the copying of older manuscript pictures. The Latin *Virgil* in the Vatican Library is the work of a Roman copyist.

The copy of the work of the Greek physician Dioscorides which was produced in Constantinople contained illustrations largely imitated from the earlier manuscript. The only innovation is a frontispiece of the sixth century showing the woman who commissioned the work. She is seen here as she is also seen on a contemporary ivory—the Princess Juliana Anicia, a great-granddaughter of Galla Placidia, ceremonially enthroned and in the company of allegorical figures of Wisdom or Discernment (holding the book) and Liberality (holding coins in her lap). There is also a genius whom the princess rewards, represented as "the passion of those whose joy it is to build up," an allusion to the princess's active interest in building, also referred to in the small scenes enclosed in the angles of the frame.

Dedicatory miniature of Juliana Anicia. Size of page, $14^5/8$ x $11^3/4$". c. 512. From the *Vienna Dioscorides,* fol. 6 verso. Ms. Med. Gr. 1, Nationalbibliothek, Vienna

CODICIBVS SACRIS HOSTILI CLADE PERVSTIS
ESDRA DO FERVENS HOC REPARAVIT OPVS

Rebecca and Eliezer at the Well. Book illumination, $12^{1}/_{4} \times 9^{7}/_{8}''$. Sixth century. From the *Vienna Genesis,* fol. 7. Ms. Theol. Gr. 31, Nationalbibliothek, Vienna

"Cassiodorus" Writing in Front of His Cupboard. Copy of a book illumination. Sixth century. Ms. Amiatinus 1, Biblioteca Laurentiana, Florence

The earliest surviving Bible illustrations are in a parchment manuscript in the Nationalbibliothek, Vienna. The sure touch in dealing with Biblical events, the refined technique of the purple tinting which gives a high solemnity to the scenes and figures, and the consistency of style are proof enough that this was not a first tentative effort to link Biblical scenes with a text. Scholars have even suggested that this may be a copy of a fourth-century manuscript. Whether or not this is so, the naturalness of movement of the bodies, their skill-ful full-dimensional portrayal, and the adoption of classical motifs such as the water-nymph with the pitcher, are all in keeping with the predilection for Antique pagan themes in the sixth century, when this work is thought to have been created. The "Cassiodorus" portrait, too, is completely in the tradition of late classical book illustration.

Earlier Jewish models have also left their stamp on certain scenes. In the page shown here, Rebecca is seen coming out of the city of Nahor (represented like a piece of theatrical scenery) to go down to the well, where she gives water from her pitcher to Abraham's servant, Eliezer. The landscape is sparsely indicated with just enough detail to locate the figures and explain the situation.

Christ's Entry into Jerusalem. Book illumination, $11^{3}/_{4} \times 10^{1}/_{4}''$. Late sixth century. From the *Codex Purpureus Rossanensis,* ▶ fol. 1 verso. Archiepiscopal Library, Rossano

In the *Vienna Genesis,* scenes from the story of Joseph are arranged as a continuous narrative in two strips. Everything takes place on a narrow piece of ground, as if at the front of a stage, with only an occasional glimpse of landscape beyond.

New Testament scenes, which could not have looked back to any Jewish antecedents, survive in two other purple-tinted manuscripts. The gospel book in Rossano has scenes of the Passion, from the raising of Lazarus to the judgment by Pilate. The illustrations do not accompany the text but have their own pages provided either with annotations or, as in this case, with textual concordances. The avoidance of the necessity to illustrate every detail allows each scene to speak with more meaning and force, and this freedom gives each scene a greater concentration within itself and allows it to make a greater impact. There is little attempt to delineate figures in the round—a reminder of the etherealized style which characterized the "Greek renaissance" of the late sixth century. So far, speculation as to the place of origin has led to no totally convincing theory, but until cogent arguments show otherwise, it is reasonable to attribute so splendid a manuscript to the capital and to circles enjoying the patronage of the court.

Joseph and His Brothers. Book illumination, $12^{1}/_{4} \times 9^{7}/_{8}''$. Sixth century. From the *Vienna Genesis,* fol. 30. Ms. Theol. Gr. 31, Nationalbibliothek, Vienna

Beheading of John the Baptist. Miniature on purple ground, $11^{3}/_{4} \times 9^{7}/_{8}''$. Sixth century. From the *Codex Sinopensis,* fol. 10, verso. Bibliothèque Nationale, Paris

The fragmentary Gospel of Saint Matthew in Paris was purchased in the nineteenth century by a French colonial official in Sinop, northern Anatolia. Their greater liveliness notwithstanding, the illustrations in this manuscript are closely akin to those of the Rossano Codex. Like the latter, they refrain from expanding on the story if this is not demanded by the subject illustrated, such as, for instance, the depiction of the inside of the prison, where John the Baptist's headless body lies. A prophet on each side holds an open scroll on which Old Testament texts, bearing on the scene of the beheading, are inscribed, making this not so much an illustration of the text as a commentary on the Old Testament.

All these Byzantine manuscripts conform with one another in their derivation from earlier prototypes, but the Latin manuscript of the Pentateuch (first five books of the Old Testament, ascribed to Moses) has a style all its own. It has whole-page miniatures comprising several scenes; on the facing page we see in continuous juxtaposition a series ranging from the expulsion from Eden to the killing of Abel. Brief sentences tell us what is going on, e.g., "Here Adam tills the soil." This method of continuous narrative anticipates, by its primitive organization of isolated elements, the medieval method of storytelling through a series of pictures. A relationship to Jewish Biblical illustrations from Dura-Europos (on the Euphrates) suggests a possible North African or Palestinian provenance.

The Story of Adam. Book illumination, 14⅝ x 13″. From the *Ashburnham Pentateuch*, fol. 6. Ms. nouv. acq. lat. 2334, Bibliothèque Nationale, Paris

The language of the *Rabula Codex* proves that it must have been a Syrian work. Here, too, the pages with pictures are separate from the text pages. This may well be explained by the monumental nature of the com-positions chosen for most of the illustrations, similar to those of apse mosaics or paintings. This is true of the *Crucifixion* shown here, in its two zones reminding us not only stylistically but also in the arrangement of the scenes of Egyptian apsidal decorations.

The importance of the few Egyptian frescoes from Bawit and Saqqara is that they give some idea of the lost decoration of the great cathedrals. All these frescoes belong to the fifth, sixth, or seventh centuries. The theme of paintings in Coptic church apses is usually an Epiphany arranged in two zones, the upper one testifying to the Godhead of Christ, the lower showing the witnesses to whom Christ manifested Himself. The Ascension of Christ introduces in the lower zone the Virgin Mary and the Apostles as witnesses to this event; in the same way, the *Crucifixion* in the upper zone of the picture from the *Rabula Codex* is affirmed in the lower zone by the three women at the Tomb, signifying that the Crucified was truly risen from the dead.

Saint Luke. Wall painting from tomb chapel of Saints Felix and Adauctus. c. 680. Catacomb of Commodilla, Rome

Also from Bawit is the wooden panel on the facing page, an early icon, showing Christ with the highly venerated warrior-saint Menas. Stilistically it is comparable with the Bawit wall paintings, so that henceforward there are criteria for defining a Syrian style. The *Rabula Codex* diverges stylistically from the two Bawit examples in its method of presenting figures; as well as showing Western influences, it is of a higher quality.

The veneration of saints, which was given its original impetus by monasticism in the territories covered by the Eastern Church, created the need to represent them as realistically as the art of late Antiquity represented the dead in mummy portraits, in order to make them the more immediately venerable. It was icons that made this form of presentation, this immediacy, possible. They were first used in the sixth century in Egypt and in Sinai and were to become the most significant artistic objects of the whole Eastern Church.

In the seventh century, Eastern Church icons were directly influenced by Western art. In the Catacomb of Commodilla in Rome, the fresco decoration in the *martyrium* of Saints Felix and Adauctus shows on a large scale mural reproductions of icons. In general style these Roman copies, in another medium, are close to the Eastern originals.

Christ and Saint Menas. Icon. Tempera on wood, $22^1/_2 \times 22^1/_2''$. Sixth century. From Bawit, Egypt. The Louvre, Paris

The art of mosaic working was at a high level of achievement in Justinian's reign, but we have very few mosaics from Christian sources dating back as far as the year 500—most of them were destroyed by the iconoclasts.

The nature of the inheritance from the mosaic artists of classical Antiquity may best be judged by studying a pavement from one of the inner courts of the Great Palace at Constantinople. There are several scenes on a white ground which combine to make a pictorially rich composition: pastoral and hunting scenes, landscapes and military groups, all with classical antecedents in mosaic. The technique is extremely subtle. For the bodies, the mosaic pieces are set so as to follow the lines of limbs and garments. The regular overlapping

*Head of a Martyr (Saint
Onesiphoros).* Detail of
dome mosaic. c. 400.
Saint George, Salonika

fan design of the white background stones forms a neutral foil against which the figures stand out perfectly, just as the purple background of some early manuscript pages throws into prominence the painted scenes. The perceptive treatment of human and animal forms, the delight in pleasing detail and in animated scenes, invite direct comparison with the Biblical illustrations of the *Vienna Genesis.*

Early Christian mosaics are well known to us from the many examples in the catacombs and in Ravenna, whereas in pre-Christian Antiquity mural mosaics were rare and confined to particular uses—for instance, they might be used for grottoes of the Muses. In Christian art, mosaic wall decoration ousted wall painting for a very long period. Instead of the dull natural stones, pieces of colored molten glass were often used, sometimes backed with gold. After the sixth century, a gold background, involving the fusion of molten glass and gold leaf, had become a characteristic feature of Christian wall mosaics. It clothed the surface with a luminous layer on which the sacred beings and scenes were displayed. Mosaic art now became an auton-omous art form with its own canons, including new rules concerning the depiction of faces and forms. It is true that saints still bore the features of heroic faces of Antiquity; but the proportions were flattened, bodies retreated behind robes, and these robes were adorned with decorative devices which served to indicate the folds. In the architectonic backgrounds, elaborate representation was abandoned in favor of flat surface patterns. For these reasons, it is not easy to decide whether the mosaics, to which the one in the illustration above belongs, date back to the time at the end of the fourth century when the building was being trans-formed into a church, or whether they are part of a later refurbishing.

The mosaic from Saint David, a modest church in a suburb of Salonika, shows, as the vision of Ezekiel, the aureoled Christ enthroned above a rainbow with the symbols of the four Evangelists, and an additional figure usually identified as Habakkuk. Since he is holding the dedicatory inscription of the church, the figure could also represent its former patron, Saint Zacharias. This is one of the earliest apse mosaics. Even as early as about 470, Salonika had churches decorated with mosaics, as a fragment from the basilica of the Acheiropoietos proves.

Not only walls and vaults, but supporting columns, arcades, and other architectural features were also decorated and emphasized with mosaics. Here a votive picture is shown: Saint Demetrius stands between the founders of the church, who thus acquaint him with their wishes. This is a worthy forerunner of all the ex-voto pictures which were to abound in subsequent ages down to our own day. The high ceremonial style of the imperial court of Justinian's era, as we have seen it at Ravenna, now becomes stiff and formalized. The folds of the garments no longer follow the lines of the body, but form an independent pattern of their own. Since Bishop John, who rebuilt the church after its destruction by fire in 625, is portrayed, we can assume that this mosaic comes from the second quarter of the seventh century.

Saint Demetrius Standing Between an Ecclesiastical and a Secular Dignatory. Mosaic on south pier of apse. c. 635. Saint Demetrius, Salonika

Mary Between Archangels. Apse mosaic. Seventh century. Panhagia Angeloktistos, Chiti

The iconoclasts' onslaught of the eighth century put an end to the period of creativity initiated by Justinian. It was not just a clash of religious attitudes; the background was to a great extent political and concerned with the imperial succession in various regions. Leo III, the Isaurian, was leader of a faction based on Anatolia in Asia Minor. Relying on his strong military position, he overthrew the weak Emperor Theodosius III and had himself proclaimed Emperor and restorer of imperial prestige in 717. In order to strengthen the power of the army against that of the monks, and out of beliefs current in Asia Minor, Leo III attacked the use of "images," more especially those of Christ Himself. The iconoclasts effaced almost all the works of art in the apses of Eastern churches. Of the few that survived, it is strange that so many should be devoted to representations of the Madonna, so much rarer in Western churches then. The favorite form was the standing Madonna with the Child held in her left arm; to the figure in this attitude the name "Hodegetria" was applied, meaning "leader" or "guide." The Virgin is shown thus in the apse of Chiti, standing between the worshiping archangels Michael and Gabriel who each carry a globe representing the universe, signifying the submission of the whole world to the power of Christ. This kind of imagery would have been so offensive to the iconoclasts that it would nearly always have been removed from the churches. In the Church of the Koimesis (Assumption) in Nicaea (Iznik), the apsidal Madonna was replaced by a Cross, and when the iconoclastic fury had died down the Cross yielded to a ninth-century Madonna.

THE MACEDONIAN RENAISSANCE AND BYZANTINE CLASSICISM

The basilica was the typical Early Christian church form in Rome and in the East in the times before the Byzantine builders replaced it with the more and more sophisticated types of plan organized round a central core. These expressed themselves in the kinds of cruciform domed church which finally came to count as the typical Byzantine form. Not unjustifiably, this has been taken for a state-planned building program. A few buildings of almost unaltered basilican form did persist until medieval times; they were not domed but had timbered roofs, as at Serrai (Serres), and all echoed Early Christian building concepts; but in the disposition of their elements these churches (for instance, in the related one at Arta, Epirus) are so closely connected with Western basilican structures of the first centuries of the Christian era, that there must have been direct influence. As a type, they appeared exclusively in the area of Byzantine influence in northern Greece, which anyhow, as the first millennium drew to a close, tended more and more to have relations with the West. This church and its mosaics, some of which remain, is therefore of little help in the reconstruction of local Byzantine mosaic art in the times of the Comneni. It belongs, as the Sicilian churches do, to a westward-looking pattern; its mosaics would appear to be imitations of work of the capital, rather than examples of metropolitan Byzantine art itself.

Serrai Cathedral, Greece. Eleventh century

By the beginning of the tenth century, the iconoclasts were no longer active. Planners and builders were able to devote themselves to the new calculations and experiments which were to culminate in the classical phase of Byzantine architecture. The prototype building was the Nea within the Great Palace precincts, the new palatine church consecrated in 881. Our knowledge of it comes only from a contemporary description and a representation of it in Basil II's *Menologium.* The upper dome and its drum rested on four freestanding piers, and the corner domes reduced the lateral thrust considerably, so that a loftier, more compact building could safely be erected. The great windows in the drum flooded the interior with light. The other buildings of this fundamental type which went up in the reign of Constantine VII Porphyrogenitus, a very active patron of the arts, have disappeared, but there is a survivor from the mid-tenth century in the little Myreleion monastery church built under Romanus I Lecapenus, regent for Constantine VII. It again follows the cruciform domed pattern, as the Nea did, but instead of the corner domes it has vaulting also on the cruciform

Budrum Cami mosque, Constantinople (Istanbul). Former Myreleion monastery church. c. 930

Church of Saint Theodore, Mistra, Greece. Eleventh century ▶

plan. Moreover, it achieves a grandiose spaciousness by eliminating internally the walls of the octagon or circle at the core of a church. A strikingly unusual external decorative feature is the series of pilasters or half-columns let into the walls to emphasize the vertical sweep of the building. The minaret, as is usually the case when it appears as part of a Constantinople church, is a fifteenth-century addition, dating from the time of the church's transformation into a mosque known as the Budrum Cami.

The basic form of a drum with four supporting piers found widespread adoption and rich interpretation in Greece. Saint Luke of Stiris, the church of Daphni, and Saint Theodore in Mistra, are all offshoots of the same basic plan. In this last example, we see the dome covering the whole span of the three aisles so that two supplementary aisle-like units had to be added, one either side, over which the lateral arc of the dome could spread its weight. The dome is so unmistakably the predominant element that even when viewed from outside it reveals most of its structural secrets. The remaining architectural elements are closely packed around the cube on which it rests and fall away from it in descending levels. The masons' work of the exterior walls is exceptionally well executed; the elaborate embellishment around the window apertures is a thirteenth-century feature. The alternation of types of material—undressed stone, ashlar, and brick—clearly has a decorative aim which is unusual in earlier Byzantine art.

Saint Luke of Stiris, Phocis, Greece. Beginning of eleventh century. Above: exterior. Right: interior with apse showing the Madonna and Child, and cupola showing the Feast of Pentecost

Saint Luke of Stiris is one of the best-preserved sacred buildings of the middle Byzantine epoch. To the right in the photograph above, there are the remains of a building said to have been begun by the patron saint, a revered ascetic and founder of this church, who died in 946. The main church with its broad dome adjoins the more ancient fabric and it was begun either by the Empress Theophano or by her son Basil II (976–1025). It was exceptionally well endowed as a place of pilgrimage and had a shrine enclosing the saint's tomb. The dome covers the three aisles and rests on four divided piers, which thus provide eight supports for the structure. Its pendentives lead the thrust of the dome down onto these supports, but since they could not take the whole weight, a new surrounding space to take buttresses was necessary.

On the outside walls of the church, there are areas of decorative stonework which seem unrelated to the structural lines: hewn stone and brick in lively horizontal patterns. The roof, with its pleasing gradation of levels, is a better indicator of the internal layout which it covers.

The loveliest mosaics of the classical Byzantine period are to be found in Greece; in this church almost all the mosaics are intact. Since the building was commissioned by the imperial house, and since the adornment of the interior was of a quality appropriate to the great imperial buildings of Justinian's time, it is reasonable to suppose that court artists made the mosaics. A comparison with the contemporary examples of Hagia Sophia lends weight to this theory.

The great dome mosaic, now destroyed, of Saint Luke of Stiris once showed a Christ Pantocrator similar to that in the Arta dome. The minor dome in front of the apse, with the Descent of the Holy Ghost, shows fairly well-preserved mosaics, and in the apse Mary Theotokos (Mother of God) is enthroned against a gold background. In the wall recesses are Fathers of the Greek Church.

Group of Apostles from the *Dormition of the Virgin*. Mosaic. Early eleventh century. Saint Luke of Stiris, Phocis, Greece

Mary Between Justinian and Constantine. Mosaic. c. 990. ▶ South Portal, Hagia Sophia, Constantinople (Istanbul)

Some students see the mosaics of Saint Luke of Stiris as the works of a provincial monastic group, but the fact that this was an imperial foundation must surely mean that all the artists came from Constantinople. There are also some stylistic peculiarities which point to Salonika.

The detail above, showing a group of Apostles, is a clear example of the stylistic features typical of Saint Luke. The method of representing individuals has been reduced to a formula, and their number is limited strictly to those required to narrate the bare events. These are calm, self-possessed beings and there is no dramatic handling of the themes anywhere. Colors are sober and concentrated in a few large monochrome areas. There is no play of light and shadow. The outlines of the colored shapes define them without lending them any three-dimensional quality. Decoration is more important than realistic representation.

We know from the lunette mosaics in the Hagia Sophia narthex that a certain style was favored in the capital at the end of the tenth century. Basil II probably commissioned these, and it is known that he deeply respected his predecessors Constantine and Justinian; with their example always in mind, he attempted to restore the empire's old frontiers. In the mosaic seen here, Constantine is carrying the city he founded and called Constantinople, and Justinian is carrying the principal church associated with him, Hagia Sophia itself. The recipient of these votive offerings is Mary Theotokos, Mother of God. These allusions to the rehabilitation of the city and the empire under Basil II may indicate a later date after his victory over the Bulgarians (1018). In the tenth and eleventh centuries, the mosaics were constantly renewed and increased in number. The new work is so closely related to the Madonna mosaic of Saint Luke of Stiris that one may postulate at least a very close dating and perhaps the same patron, though not necessarily the same provenance.

The high flowering of the classical style in Byzantine mosaic art of the eleventh century is still to be sought in Greece. The formerly fortified monastic church of Daphni near Athens is, in its basic plan, closely related to Saint Luke of Stiris and is probably also an imperial foundation. The decoration of the church interior is closely connected with styles in the capital, so a date of 1100 for it is probably correct. Very few other mosaics of this period survive in what was then metropolitan Byzantium. Daphni is highly important in the history of art because at the time of its building Byzantine influences were changing the nature of Russian art and the Daphni mosaics show just those nuances and gradations of style which are the basis of the mosaics of Saint Michael's cathedral in Kiev.

This is an art capable of conveying God's divine majesty in the great dome and then moving easily into a simple narrative style with human figures that hark back to the forms of Greek Antiquity. It is a manifestation of a new ideal of Greek humanism, an ideal much to the taste of the Comnenus period, as expressed in the writings of Michael Psellus. The Daphni mosaics cover the interior with representations of all the great festivals of the Christian year. In the Christmas episode here, the landscape is built up in gentle, relief-like undulations; the contours of the two-dimensional figures are rendered by a lineal treatment to lift them out of the darker zones. Grace and eloquence combine to create an autonomous and transcendental world of images, which one would scarcely guess belonged to an iconographic scheme dictated by the architectural elements of the church, being almost an integral part of them. The artistic technique serves this new concept well: the mosaic pieces are smaller than usual, giving a greater feeling of movement, finer gradations of color, a more subtle impression of relief, and a softer characterization of facial expression.

◄ *Christ Pantocrator.* Dome mosaic. c. 1100. Monastery church, Daphni, near Athens

The Nativity. Pendentive mosaic. c. 1100. Monastery church, Daphni, near Athens

The Transfigura-tion. Pendentive mosaic. c. 1100. Monastery church, D a p h n i, n e a r Athens

There is a new ideal of beauty in Daphni, and a new narrative form has been cleverly worked out, but the artist is still faithful to certain traditions. The Christian artists of the East had evolved an unvarying formula for representations of the Transfiguration, and even in the thirteenth and fourteenth centuries their heirs saw no reason for varying it.

Christ, white-robed in a mandorla with radiant beams, stands on a mountain with Moses and Elijah to the left and right and with John prostrate at his feet, and Peter and James kneeling at either side. All of them, as witnesses of God's affirmation of His Son, are touched by beams of light. Such a presentation in itself became an object of worship, so that it often appeared entirely on its own, detached from the cycle of Christian festivals and major events with which churches were decorated. It appeared, for instance, as a mosaic icon of the thirteenth century (see facing page), now in Paris. Representations of Christ, of Mary, of the Crucifixion, and of the Annunciation were the chosen subjects of small works used as devotional pictures—miniature examples of a genre which, in keeping with its nature, was usually intended for impressive murals. In the second half of the tenth century, the actual placing of the mosaic pieces became a finer art, and this led to an ever greater independence of the individual parts of the composition in relation to the overall decorative scheme. Inevitably this technical development, after about 1050, was applied to smaller panel mosaics. The oldest known example of this art form dates from about 1060 and was made on order of a member of the ruling Comnenus house. From that time until well into the fifteenth century, mosaic artists produced quantities of icons of this kind, as well as the great murals.

The Transfiguration. Mosaic icon, 20¹/₂ x 14¹/₈″. Beginning of thirteenth century. The Louvre, Paris

Detailed pictorial mosaics also contributed to the decoration of churches in the form of ex-votos. For these there is a long tradition going back ultimately to the portraits of sovereigns in San Vitale, Ravenna. In eleventh-century Constantinople, there was one particular theme which recommended itself for the ex-voto: Christ enthroned between the Emperor and the Empress. Hagia Sophia, as the court church, received these offerings. The mosaic showing Christ between Constantine IX Monomachus and Empress Zoë was completed between 1028 and 1034. Parts of it were chipped away in 1041 and in 1042 it was refashioned with several changes. These few dates show how Byzantine palace and state politics can be mirrored in a work of art and its vicissitudes. The Empress Zoë had been married to Romanus III Argyrus, who was murdered in 1034. The mosaic was already in existence then. Michael V became Emperor in 1041, deposing Zoë, but a popular revolt restored her to the throne and soon afterward she married Constantine IX Monomachus. On the renewal in 1042 of the mosaic, damaged by Michael V, Romanus' likeness was replaced by that of the new Emperor, Constantine. The style is very similar to that of mosaics in Hagia Sophia belonging to the ninth and tenth centuries.

Mosaic icons were used also in private devotions; most of them are reproductions of themes already worked out on the walls of major churches. Christ with the Gospels in His hand and the Cross in a nimbus behind His head was a frequently used subject for dome mosaics, as at Daphni, for example (page 160). When mosaic art moved toward the greater refinement of the late tenth century, the representations of Christ became less austere, less sacerdotal.

Christ Pantocrator Between the Emperor Constantine IX Monomachus and the Empress Zoë. 1028–34. Hagia Sophia, Constantinople (Istanbul)

Christ the Compassionate. Mosaic icon, 29$^{1}/_{4}$ × 22$^{5}/_{8}$". c. 1100. State Museums, Berlin

Vision of Ezekiel. Book illumination, 16⁷/₈ x 11⁷/₈″. 867–86. *Homilies of Gregory of Nazianzus,* fol. 438 verso. Ms. gr. 510, Bibliothèque Nationale, Paris

David and His Choirs. Ninth century. *Topographia Christiana of CosmasIndicopleustes,* fol. 63 verso. Ms. Gr. 699, Biblioteca Vaticana, Rome

The beginning of post-iconoclastic art is shown in the extraordinary popularity of book illumination. It was the finest fruit of the classical revival under the Macedonian Emperors. Once again, border and landscape motifs of late Antiquity were taken up, as were depictions of animals and human beings and the arrangement of scenes characteristic of Early Christian art. The *Homilies* of Saint Gregory of Nazianzus, now in Paris, may be dated between 867 and 886 on account of the dedication to Basil I.

Cosmas Indicopleustes composed his *Christian Topography* in the sixth century. The earliest known illustrated copy is a ninth-century one and it clearly follows a predecessor belonging to Cosmas' own time, whose illuminations may, in turn, have been based on yet earlier models. Even so, this manuscript, in its strictness of form reminiscent of Justinian art, prepares the way for that of the tenth century.

The *Joshua Roll* is the greatest work of book illustration of the so-called "Macedonian renaissance." Dates and provenance are disputed, but it was probably commissioned by Constantine VII Porphyrogenitus, who was a fervent supporter of the return to classical models. The work is a manuscript designed to unroll sideways, and the various episodes of a story are frequently set in a long row for continuity. As the illustrations have close resemblances to those of late Antiquity, many attempts have been made to relate them to earlier styles, which, in another medium, chose the continuous band of episodes for telling a story—for example,

The Archangel Michael. Detail of illustration on facing page

Joshua and the Angel. Part of the ▶ *Joshua Roll.* Height 12¹/₂″, overall length of roll 33′. First half of tenth century. Ms. Gr. 431, Biblioteca Vaticana, Rome

Trajan's Column. Professor Weitzmann believes that insertions have been made between neighboring scenes for the sake of continuity, and are not part of the original scroll. The backward-looking style and the unusual form of the completed roll have persuaded several scholars that it belongs to the sixth or seventh centuries, but there is no agreement on this. The mainly military events in which the Biblical hero Joshua was involved complement ideally the warlike preoccupations of Constantine VII in Palestine.

The illustrator confines himself to lightly and sensitively colored drawings. With economy of line, the figures are given their individual characteristics, and with an incredibly sure touch, movement is conveyed through anatomical accuracy allied with bold assertion. At the same time, it was quite possible to show the same person twice over in a given scene. For instance, we see Joshua conversing with the angel, yet at the same moment he is shown in a fashion typical of the mid-Byzantine period (as Beckwith points out) falling to the ground before the angel in the attitude of "proskynesis." The figures go about their various concerns in front of a city wall with trees about it, and the seated city-goddess identifies the place as Jericho. Interpretation of gesture and of features of the landscape, and not least the consonance of garment fold and bodily stance, are so close to what we have seen in the *Homilies of Gregory of Nazianzus* that a tenth-century origin can hardly be doubted. Whether the panoramic breadth of the scenes and the method of continuous narrative really are peculiar to this period, or whether they were taken over from some earlier convention which has left no other traces, must remain an unsettled question. We cannot refer to any comparable work.

It is the fourteen illustrations of the *Paris Psalter* that furnish the most unmistakable evidence of borrowings from classical Antiquity by the court painters of the tenth century. David as the new Orpheus bewitches the animals with his harp playing and his attendant nymph becomes the divinity of Bethlehem. Behind every detail of the figures and of the landscape is a prototype which has its roots not only in pre-iconoclastic works but also far back in the wall paintings of late Antiquity, known only to us from Roman copies in Pompeiian frescoes. But the relationship of the individual forms of the *Paris Psalter* to the miniatures of the *Homilies of Gregory of Nazianzus* leaves us in no doubt that both were created at the same time. The differences probably go back only to variations in the models they followed.

In the so-called "Palace Psalters" of the tenth century, the draping of garments and the method of depicting persons show certain resemblances to mural conventions of classical times. Even so, close relationships with the mosaics of imperial church founders, which present the individuals much more austerely, keep them well in the mainstream of Byzantine tradition reaching back to Justinian's day. Here, David is seen between personifications of his two most resounding attributes, Wisdom and Prophecy, rather like Justinian standing between his two counselors, or Christ with a member of the imperial family either side of Him. This stylistic tendency was further encouraged under Basil II (976–1025) when he moved the Scriptorium from the Great Palace to the Blachernae Palace.

◄ *David with His Flocks*. Book illumination, 14¹/₈ × 10¹/₄″. Early tenth century. *Paris Psalter*, fol. 1 verso. Ms. gr. 139, Bibliothèque Nationale, Paris

David Standing Between Wisdom and Prophecy. From an illuminated *Psalter*. Eleventh century. Ms. Gr. 381, Biblioteca Vaticana, Rome

Translation of the Relics of Saint John Chrysostom to the Church of the Holy Apostles, Constantinople. Book illumination, 14¼ x 11⅛". c. 985. From the *Menologium* of Basil II. Ms. Gr. 1613, Biblioteca Vaticana, Rome

Basil II instructed his palace artists to compile a book of the life stories of the most important saints—a *Menologium*. A book of this kind would have an entry for each day of the year and an illustration touching on the events from the Bible and the martyrs' lives mentioned in the liturgy for that day. The portion of Basil's *Menologium* which has come down to us covers the ecclesiastical year from September to February, contains in all thirty-four miniatures, and (this was not customary in Byzantium) has an artist's signature in the margin of each. The artists used their own powers of observation and made their own discoveries. Whenever there was scope for it, they drew churches in Constantinople—it must be borne in mind that the history of the relics in them was very much the matter of the *Menologium*. One illustration shows the carrying of the relics of Saint John Chrysostom into the Church of the Holy Apostles, which is now destroyed but which, as contemporary writings, for example, those of Constantine of Rhodes (c. 931–44), confirm, is faithfully represented with its five domes.

A change of style was initiated by the Blachernae School. Colors grew darker, form ceased to be the main concern. The simple, clear, narrative style and the exact rendering of illustrative detail were especially well suited to the functions of the historian.

The stronger colors of the Blachernae School very soon became general for manuscript illustrations commissioned by the court and are important for their effect on the art of the twelfth-century miniaturists. The *Ascension* from a collection of writings on the life of the Virgin shows how effectively a rich architectural framework could enhance the whole.

The Ascension. Book illumination, 9 x 6⅜". First half of twelfth century. From *Homilies of the Virgin* by the monk James ▶ of Kokkinobaphos, fol. 3 verso. Ms. gr. 1208, Bibliothèque Nationale, Paris

Paten with image of Christ. Alabaster, gold cloisonné, and precious stones, diameter 13⅜″. Eleventh century. Cathedral treasury, Saint Mark's, Venice

Chalice. Onyx with silver-gilt setting, ▶ enamel, and pearls. Second half of twelfth century. From Constantinople. Cathedral treasury, Saint Mark's, Venice

Chalice of the Emperor Romanus. Onyx with silver-gilt setting, pearls, and enamel, height 8¾″. c. 940. Cathedral treasury, Saint Mark's, Venice

Once again, the post-iconoclastic reawakening of the artist, together with the revived interest in classical forms under the Macedonian dynasty, must be mentioned for their far-reaching effects on the applied arts. Church plate, which also had its imperial connotations, has survived mainly in Venice. In the treasury of Saint Mark's cathedral are more than thirty precious Byzantine chalices of the tenth and eleventh centuries, many with the names of church founders or patrons, making it possible to date them. The chalice inscribed with the name "Romanus," probably Romanus I Lecapenus who came to the throne as co-regent in 919, demonstrates the enameling technique at its most successful. It may be seen on the *Limburg Staurotheca* (page 177) and the alabaster paten in Saint Mark's. The framing of medallions or plaques with pearl

beading is an ornamental device frequently used in this group and is for us typical of the tenth century. Alabaster, onyx, sardonyx, jasper, and other gems were mounted in silver and applied to chalices and bowls. The vessels were used for the Mass. "Take, eat, this is My body" is inscribed on the alabaster paten, used for the consecrated Host. A sardonyx chalice in Saint Mark's has a pendant inscription, "Drink ye all of this, for this is My blood." The enameling shows that it belongs to the same group, all of the tenth or early eleventh centuries.

The Limburg reliquary of the True Cross is probably the finest example of tenth-century enameling. The inscription shows that it was a commission from Basil Proedrus, son of Romanus I Lecapenus, and must have been made in about 964. In 1204, this precious reliquary was brought back as booty from the Holy Land by the crusader Heinrich von Ulmen. The ornament of the borders, the fine draftsmanship, and the style of the drapery relate the figurative enamels to the work of court miniaturists of about the year 1000.

It is to the time of Constantine IX Monomachus, and the first panels of the *Pala d'Oro* of Saint Mark's, thus to the eleventh century, that we can attribute the somewhat provincial and oddly alien enameled figures of the reliquary of the True Cross in Esztergom, Hungary, still displaying clearly its relic worked into a cross form. The cross has two transverse pieces and resembles all reliquary crosses of the period. On the back of the Limburg reliquary, the same type of cross is found.

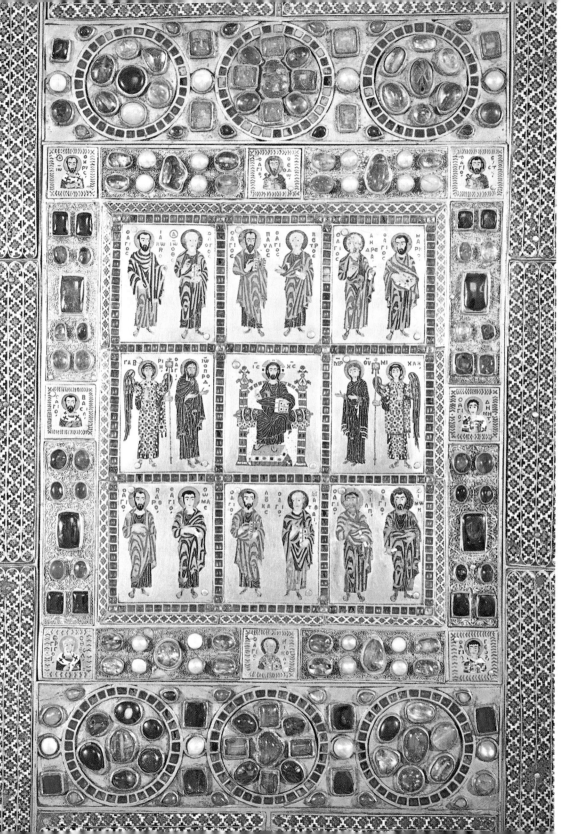

Book cover with archangel. Gold cloisonné with enamel inlays, 18⁷/₈ x 14¹/₈″. Eleventh century. Cathedral treasury, Saint Mark's, Venice

Toward the end of the tenth century, many chased gold and silver pieces were created. In the example on the facing page, enameling has been added to enrich both the main picture of chased silver and the framing edges.

One of the favorite subjects for book covers was the "Anastasis," Christ's descent to Limbo, which in Byzantium was a concept representing the Resurrection. The thirteenth-century book cover in Venice has a border of theological allusions personified by prophets and teachers. The "Hetoimasia," or empty throne, waiting for the time to come when the Son of God will occupy it, complements the picture of the Conqueror of Hell. Similar items in chased silver were made in Italy in the fourteenth century. The Venice cover involves the possibility that a North Italian silversmith copied a Byzantine model.

Book cover with "Anastasis." Silver gilt, 13 × 7⁷/₈". Thirteenth century. Biblioteca Marciana, Venice

Pala d'Oro. Altar. Gold cloisonné inlaid with precious stones, 83½ x 131½″. Eleventh–fourteenth centuries. Saint Mark's, Venice

The most splendid example of Byzantine enamelwork is the *Pala d'Oro* in Saint Mark's, Venice. The Doge, Pietro II Orseolo (991–1009), ordered a golden altar from Constantinople at the rebuilding of the cathedral. There are stylistic resemblances to the Holy Crown of Hungary and the crown of Constantine IX Monomachus (page 182) which leave no doubt that the ancient enamel plaques seen today on the altar are not the original ones. They must belong to a second commission at the time of a subsequent stage of rebuilding between 1063 and 1094. The Doge Ordelafo Falier (1102–18) ordered a new altar frontal from Constantinople, and from this piece comes the central panel of the present *Pala d'Oro*. It shows Christ as Pantocrator surrounded by the Evangelists. Above is the empty throne, the "Hetoimasia," with attendant seraphim and cherubim. The row of figures below Christ Enthroned is no longer intact; originally it included the Mother of God with representations of the royal pair then reigning—Alexius I Comnenus (1081–1118) and the Empress Irene—and a portrait of the Doge Ordelafo Falier. Now only three plaques remain showing Mary, the Empress Irene, and the Doge.

In 1209, the Doge Pietro Zani had six large enamel plaques added, representing the great feasts of the Church's year. These were not made to order, but had been looted from one of the great Byzantine churches, probably Hagia Sophia itself, in 1204. It was not until 1345, under the distinguished Doge Andrea Dandolo,

The Empress Irene. Plaque from the *Pala d'Oro.* Gold cloisonné. 1081–1118. Saint Mark's, Venice

that the *Pala d'Oro* was restored to its present condition. The central panel is substantially as it was in the time of Ordelafo Falier in its arrangement. New plaques were added, some actually made in Venice, and a few from the first altar. All parts were then enclosed in a Gothic frame.

Crown of Constantine IX Monomachus. Gold inlaid with enamel, largest piece, 4¹/₂ × 2″. 1042–50. National Museum, Budapest

Crowns were the kind of gift Byzantine Emperors liked to send to rulers and regents in allied lands, hoping thereby to ensure their loyalty. We know that some time between 1074 and 1077 Michael VII Parapinakes sent a crown to the wife of King Geza I of Hungary which was later refashioned into the famous "Crown of Saint Stephen." Similar crowns were sent to Russia and Turkey. In 1860, a Hungarian farmworker at Nyitra Ivanka turned up seven enamel plaques from a crown with his plow and they were given to the National Museum in Budapest. The one with the Emperor's likeness on it was inscribed, "Constantine, Emperor of the Romans, Monomachus." The two Empresses are identified as Zoë and Theodora. The other plaques are decorated with dancers and allegorical figures, and all the figures are surrounded by vines with perching birds. The crown can only have been commissioned after Constantine IX had become Emperor through his marriage to Zoë and must have been completed before Zoë's death. This dates it somewhere between 1042 and 1050. At this period, Hungary was ruled by King Andrew I, a firm ally of Byzantium, who had close ties with both Constantinople and Russia. One of Constantine's daughters had married the Russian ruler whose sister, Anastasia, was the wife of Andrew I himself.

Constantine IX Monomachus was one of the key figures of Byzantium's classical period. An outstanding patron of the arts, he founded an imposing monastic church at Nea Moni, in Chios. Ancient literature and classical models were very important for the figurative arts. The story is told of how Constantine, married to an Empress of advancing years, appeared in public with his Caucasian mistress. The resulting court gossip went down in history as an example of the benefits of a classical education. A courtier is supposed to have called out, "It is no shame . . .," which everyone at once recognized as a celebrated piece from the *Iliad* in which one of Helen's courtiers says, "It is no shame for men to come to strife over such a woman."

The few surviving examples of secular art show that, as well as sacred themes, mythological subjects were quite usual. Official palace art, however, was not distinct from sacred art, and its subject matter and style were those of the Christian art of Byzantium. On his scepter the Emperor subordinated himself to his Lord, Jesus Christ, or declared himself vassal of the Mother of God, but he did not omit his claim, however, to be numbered among the hosts of angels and archangels. In this fragment of a scepter with an inscription referring to Leo VI, the Emperor and the Archangel Gabriel are identically dressed and have similar insignia. In the upper zone, above each of the three figures, are apselike niches. The scepter was made just after the end of iconoclasm but has all the heaviness of pre-iconoclastic art. It stands at the very beginning of the revival of the figurative arts which was to lead to Byzantine classicism in the following century.

Fragment of a scepter showing Mary crowning the Emperor Leo VI. Ivory. 886–912. State Museums, Berlin

Mythological scenes on a casket. Ivory, height 4½″. Eleventh century, Cluny Museum, Paris

The revival of interest in the classical tradition in the tenth century made itself felt, too, in the art of ivory carving. Ivory pieces were not particularly sought after as booty in war, since they could not be transformed like precious metals into other forms of wealth. This explains why a comparatively large number of ivories dealing with secular subjects survived. There is a particularly interesting group of ivory caskets known as "rosette caskets," from the decoration that they all have round their edges. Almost all of them have decorative features drawn from mythology, but one small group has Biblical episodes, for the most part involving Joshua, which makes it possible to guess at the source of the craftsmen's themes. These Joshua episodes quite palpably, and with startling exactitude, match those of the *Joshua Roll* (pages 168f.). Since this roll is seen as a copy of an Early Christian manuscript, and since the other representations on the caskets show certain similarities with tenth-century copies of models from late Antiquity, manuscripts of late Antiquity and of the Early Christian period suggest themselves as sources for this whole group of caskets.

The finest among them is the large, flat-topped *Veroli Casket* from the cathedral treasury of Veroli, now in the Victoria and Albert Museum. All the carvings here have to do with one aspect or another of Eros and his powers. On the lid, Cupids surround scenes of the Rape of Europa and of Hercules playing his lyre. They also flit through the scenes showing Bellerophon and Peirene and the Sacrifice of Iphigenia. They perform a pantomime around Ares and Aphrodite and tame lions and deer. Every scene has its parallels in classical art and manuscript illustrations of the tenth century. And—a conclusive point—in the Rape of Europa episode there is a peculiarly irrelevant group of men throwing stones, copied directly from the *Joshua Roll.*

This relationship with a manuscript which was produced in the Great Palace at Constantinople has led John Beckwith to enquire into the reasons for the making of the casket. He concluded that the art-loving Emperor Constantine VIII (969–1028) had it made as a present for his daughter Zoë.

The Cluny Museum casket, of similar size, shows garlanded heads alternating with the border rosettes characteristic of the group. In small, metope-like fields, mostly in pairs, there are mythological scenes with fabulous creatures, and on the large lid surface a more popular scene, a battle. The illustration opposite shows the centaur Nessus abducting Deianira from Hercules, and also the Rape of Ganymede by Zeus, who has changed himself into an eagle. Although it clearly belongs to the same group as the *Veroli Casket,* the Paris one is difficult to date. The stylistic development of the group is not known; differences in treatment between the lid carvings and the side carvings lead to further difficulties, but an eleventh-century date seems the most probable.

So-called *Veroli Casket.* Ivory, 4¹/₂ x 16″. Tenth–eleventh centuries. Victoria and Albert Museum, London

The Tower of Babel. Mosaic from the first bay of the narthex. Saint Mark's, Venice

Saint Mark's, Venice. Exterior. 1042-71

THE SPREAD OF BYZANTINE ART IN THE WEST

The principal church of Venice, Saint Mark's, followed a Byzantine pattern and workers from Constantinople were brought in to build it. At least the first stages of the mosaics were carried out by artists from the East, and Saint Mark's is today the chief example of Byzantine church decoration of the twelfth century. In the early ninth century, the first building was closely modeled on Justinian's church of the Holy Apostles. After the fire of 976 had made a rebuilding necessary, the church of the Apostles, which had meanwhile been rebuilt by Basil II, was once more taken as the model. The Byzantine five-domed cruciform plan found many imitations of various kinds in the West. The church of the Apostles, Saint Mark's itself, and Saint Front de Périgueux all have domes over the crossing and over the four arms which form the Greek cross of the ground plan. In the East generally, particularly at Mount Athos, there were numerous adaptations of this plan. Saint Mark's shows it in its purest form.

Not only were builders from Constantinople brought to Venice, but there were other imports too. Finished stonework and ornament, particularly capitals, were brought over. As in Sicily, Venice also took over the Byzantine concept of the religious function of an interior and its decoration. No other basic architectural plan lent itself so well to ambitious and extensive mosaic decoration. There were five domes with their vast inner shells supported on their conspicuous and elegant pendentives and there were the surfaces of great arches and gallery walls awaiting the mosaic artist. The pictures were arranged according to their importance in the ecclesiastical year and according to the dictates of hagiology. So, against a golden background which caught the light from the apertures in the dome, and sent it shimmering downward into the interior, the figures of the Gospel appeared to the believers as a part of the liturgy itself, a liturgy taking place not only at fixed times in the church, but at all times in the dome above. It is a later reflection of this outlook which has come down to us in the mosaics of Saint Mark's in a completeness such as is found nowhere in the whole of the Byzantine East.

Pillars and arches are clad in fine marble, the upper walls have facings of stone from Byzantium, and in the barrel vaulting over the aisles Biblical episodes are depicted. The events of the greatest spiritual or theological importance are placed on the hemispherical vaults of the domes against a ground of gold. Angels and archangels in the pendentives support the dome with its representations of the great festivals of the Christian year; Christ Pantocrator is enthroned in the apse.

The first mosaics at Saint Mark's were certainly made by Greco-Byzantine artists. When the church was rebuilt, the Doge Domenico Selvo (1071–84) had mosaic artists brought from Constantinople. Their work was

Scenes from Genesis. Dome ▶ mosaic in narthex. Thirteenth century. Saint Mark's, Venice

Saint Mark's, Venice. Interior. 1042–71

almost totally consumed in a fire of 1106—only a few remnants have come to light during reconstructions. All the other mosaics are later than 1106 and reflect the most varied styles and influences. The main domes, for the most part, still go back to the work of twelfth-century artists; the conquest of Constantinople did nothing to break cultural links between the two cities. As well as a Latin emperor in Byzantium there was a Latin patriarch who was a Venetian. If the work of this period is characterized by greater compactness and economy, this is no criticism of the talents of the Byzantine artists, since they were being exposed to Western influences from the art of the Duecento.

The Latin rulers took over the reins of government in Byzantium in 1204. At this time, the artists at Saint Mark's were setting up the mosaics in the domes of the narthex, including scenes from the books of Moses; all the Creation or Genesis episodes there derive, with little variation, from a pre-iconoclastic Bible illustration known from a manuscript in the British Museum. The dome scene shown above has few counterparts in Western art of the time. For instance, in the middle field, Christ is seen as Creator, with six angels who represent the six days of creation, so that Christ Himself is the seventh. The inscriptions are in Latin and prove that the idea and its symbolism are Romano-Christian in origin.

Miracle of Moses in the Wilderness. Mosaic in an apsidal recess in the narthex. Thirteenth–fourteenth centuries. Saint Mark's, Venice

Palatine chapel (Capella Palatina). Twelfth century. Royal palace (Palazzo Reale), Palermo ▶

Western forms were progressively assimilated. Realism in the narration of events manifested itself practically in the greater richness of detail in each individual part of a picture. But this did not break up the basic idea of the Biblical scene in front of a gold ground, so that, surrounded by the great areas of gold, the smaller groups of figures appeared with their own characteristic and vigorous movement. Byzantine conventions are isolated and transformed into individual episodes in naturalistic settings.

Roger II (1130–54) was crowned by the antipope Anacletus II as Norman King of Sicily, and he at once imported Byzantine artists to his court in Palermo, so that the churches of his new empire might be endowed with the distinction and beauty of the famous churches of Byzantium. He also ordered the building of a palatine chapel, with a three-aisled basilican plan of Western type, but with a dome over the emphasized crossing. All the wall surfaces above the pillars, and indeed right up to the timbered roof, are adorned with mosaic designs, both abstract and figurative, culminating in the dome mosaic of Christ Pantocrator encircled by angels. The photograph on the facing page shows the view of the nave from the chancel. In later times, the mosaics were considerably altered both in style and in theme.

Decorative mosaics in the *Camera di Ruggiero*. c. 1170. Royal palace (Palazzo Reale), Palermo

In the same palace at Palermo there is a room, unconnected with the chapel, with mosaic decoration. Since it lies in that part of the palace planned by Roger II, it is known as the *Camera di Ruggiero* ("Roger's Room") or the *Sala Normanna* ("Norman Room"). All the surfaces of the cruciform vault are covered with mosaics: some parts of the ceiling mosaic are purely geometrical, and some are covered with plant forms developed into scrolls or other patterns forming borders to medallions enclosing heraldic animals. The strictly symmetrical designs on the walls are more Arabic than Byzantine in inspiration and there are occasional faint echoes of classical Antiquity. Stylistically, they bear no resemblance to the mosaics in the sacred edifices and there are no formal elements in common.

Santa Maria dell'Amiraglio—the "Admiral's Church of the Mother of God"—is the nearest approach to a Byzantine church to be built in Sicily in the twelfth century. It is now known as the Martorana church. The High Admiral George of Antioch, who founded it, was of Greek and Syrian parentage. In 1112, he offered his services to the royal court of Palermo, achieving the rank of "Ammiratus Ammiratorum" in 1132. This meant, in practice, that he was commander-in-chief of all the fighting forces. The church was completed before his death in 1151, and the dedication is verified by a charter signed by Roger in 1143. The ecclesiastics and nuns of the monastery attached to the church were all of the Greek Orthodox faith, the encouragement of which was essential to Roger II's policy in his quarrels with Pope Innocent II. It was not until the fifteenth century that the church was attached to the Benedictine monastery founded in 1146 by Manfred of Martorana, from which its present name comes.

The ground plan is that of the smaller Byzantine cruciform churches, though the layout was altered by later rebuildings, some of which obliterated certain parts of the mosaic decoration. Nineteenth-century restoration work is to be thanked for the present state of the building, which is not far removed from the original scheme.

The *Dormition of the Virgin* on the western arch of the nave, adjoining the crossing, clearly illustrates the course of development. After that at Daphni, this is the oldest large-scale rendering of this theme. In the harmony between the figures and the architecture, this *Dormition* closely resembles the manuscript illustrators' schematic convention for the same scene. The mosaic has been considerably restored, but in such a way that the original intention and effect are still perfectly clear. This work played an important part in the dissemination of this scene in the West, hardly ever depicted before then.

Dormition of the Virgin. Mosaic. c. 1151. Santa Maria dell'Amiraglio (Martorana), Palermo

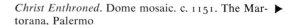

Angel. Vault mosaic. c. 1151. The Martorana, Palermo

East of the nave crossing, the high vault shows the two archangels Gabriel and Michael who, in the Capella Palatina, flanked the empty throne which, however, is absent here in the Martorana. Here, too, they belong to the decorative scheme of the great dome in which that of the rest of the church finds its climax. There is a full-length figure of Christ Pantocrator enthroned and imparting a blessing. The words from John 8: 12, "I am the light of the world," which also distinguish the Pantocrator in the Capella Palatina and in Cefalù Cathedral, are on the outer edge of the medallion encircling Him, bordering which are four adoring angels. In the drum of the dome are eight Prophets holding scrolls, and in the four pendentives between the windows, the four Evangelists. The thematic sequence is continued in the two vaults either side (each with a group of four Apostles), in the apse with the two archangels, and in the nave with the *Nativity* and the *Dormition of the Virgin.* The Martorana incorporates in a sense the whole Capella Palatina pageant on a less lavish scale in mosaics similar in scope to those of Cefalù. Of all the buildings in the new Norman-French empire in Sicily, these three owe most to the mosaic workers of Byzantium who must obviously have moved their workshops there and settled down. The color effects and harmonies achieved under their supervision in the Martorana powerfully influenced later mosaic artists of the island, mostly native Sicilians. The same style prevailed for the second phase of the Capella Palatina and later still at Monreale. But it was the magnificent

mosaic display in Cefalù Cathedral which, in its themes and its imaginative approach to them, set the standard for the work in Palermo.

There is not much of the typically Byzantine church plan to be seen in Cefalù Cathedral; there is no dome, so the Pantocrator theme has to be accommodated in the apse (see page 196). There, Christ appears as the Light of the World, as the Way and the Life, above Mary who, with four archangels, stands over the apse window. The Apostles, in two rows, are lower down. Beyond one or two portrayals of saints and a vault of angels, no other mosaics from the time of the church's foundation are left. The newly founded see had come to nothing by the end of Roger II's reign, and although he had earlier appointed Cefalù to be his burial place, he was actually buried in Palermo.

Christ Pantocrator. Apse mosaic. 1148. Cathedral, Cefalù, Sicily

The founding and the subsequent status of the cathedral of Monreale likewise depended to some extent upon political considerations, certainly upon internal politics, under William II, to whom the title of Sanctissimus Rex was granted. With the concurrence of Pope Alexander III, the founding of the basilica provided a kind of counterweight to the overpowerful English Bishop of Palermo who had allied himself with the nobility.

This enormous church, about one hundred yards long, is a transept basilica of the late Roman type with a flat, domeless roof. The apse decoration follows the Cefalù pattern. The work was begun in William II's lifetime, that is to say before 1189, as is proved by the coronation and consecration mosaic, but we can only guess at the date of its completion; scholars disagree in their estimates of the relative proportions of Byzantine and Sicilian workmanship here.

Apse mosaics. End of twelfth century. Basilica, Monreale, Sicily ▶

The Latin inscription in the mosaic reads:

DIX YSAAC AD FILIV SVV ESAV SVMEAR
MA TVA TEGREDE FORA CV VENATV ALIQD
APPHEDI FAC IDE PVLMTV VT COMEDA
DICA T AN OLMORIAR

The Apostle Peter. Apse mosaic. End
of twelfth century. Basilica, Monreale

Isaac and Esau. Mosaic in northern arcade of
nave. End of twelfth century. Basilica, Monreale

In the two Monreale side apses are enthroned the two leading Apostles claimed as national saints by the Normans. They have an exceptionally exalted place near the patron saint and the Blessed Virgin. Moreover, their life stories are the most meticulously detailed in the lunette series devoted to the lives of the Apostles. The artists had particular problems to solve, since the imposing apse figures, set so close to narrative scenes on a far smaller scale, called for much broader treatment in larger mosaic pieces. The customary range of symbols could not be used and for the Apostles there were no precedents, unlike the Pantocrator customary in domes. The tentative approach is shown not only in the lines of the heads and faces but also (in comparison with the recumbent Isaac) in the peculiarly unconvincing folds of the garment enveloping Peter.

In the smaller mosaics, the artists had to use all their ingenuity to fit personages into architecturally predetermined fields. Buildings in the background indicate the point of departure for each episode. Groups of figures are established to illustrate the stories from start to finish, and two events may be tellingly combined in a single scene—for instance, Isaac sending out Esau while Rebecca spies on them from behind a curtain, while in the same picture Esau appears again, this time out hunting. In the next area, there is a similar example of apparently simultaneous actions in two different places: Esau is still hunting and is therefore outside the dwelling; Rebecca, whom we also see, is busy using her cunning to secure from Isaac his blessing for Jacob and is therefore inside the building. The middle distance is emphatically marked and undulating hill shapes pull the composition together. The combination of buildings and landscape makes for spatial unity.

199

LATE BYZANTINE ART

In the year 1261, Michael VIII Palaeologus entered Constantinople and founded a new dynasty of Byzantine rulers which was to retain power for almost two hundred years. For sixty years at least, the progressive decline of the Empire was halted and the new dynasty was able to keep alive a consciousness of statehood and of national culture, in spite of the continuous Turkish threat. Byzantine humanism was revived with notable vigor under Andronicus (1282–1328) and his two counselors Nicephorus Choumnus and Theodorus Metochites, a humanism of Platonic inspiration which introduced into the nation a secular tone which was quite new and which gave artists fresh purpose and direction. Theodorus Metochites undertook the building of the Chora church (Kariye Cami) adjoining the palace, and on the core of an older building dating back to Theodosius he erected a new outer narthex with small domes and bedecked the whole interior with sumptuous mosaic decoration. This is a magnificent testimony to the Palaeologan humanism exhibited in contemporary writings. All the dome and lunette mosaics of the narthex are relatively well preserved, and between 1948 and 1958 they were restored by the Byzantine Institute under M. P. Underwood, so that they may now once more be seen in all the splendor of their color. A cycle of Biblical scenes within a rich, decorative pattern, with all kinds of fantastic animal shapes, shows a marked preference for classical and Early Christian forms. In choice of themes, there is a return to the post-iconoclastic Byzantine tradition but with more attention paid to the human aspect, so that we are reminded of the later mosaics in Saint Mark's.

◀ Saint Saviour in Chora (Kariye Cami), Constantinople (Istanbul). Twelfth–fourteenth centuries

Dome mosaic. c. 1315–20. Kariye Cami, Constantinople (Istanbul)

Christ Pantocrator. Mosaic above entry to outer narthex. 1300–1320. Kariye Cami, Constantinople (Istanbul)

The Pantocrator over the outer-narthex entrance might almost persuade us that we are in the period of the erection of Giotto's Arena Chapel at Padua, a time when the representation of God was not much unlike that of man and was a matter of freedom for the artist. The mosaic artist here has depicted well-rounded pitchers in the spandrel scene, has presented the buildings accurately, and has harmonized the various elements in a rich color scheme. The composition has been skillfully extended into the surrounding corners of the vault, taking advantage of the extra space to include further decorative detail.

The Nativity scene exhibits a new awareness and exploitation of detail, as is shown especially by the washing of the newborn Child. Joseph is sympathetically treated, rather in the tradition of Giotto's treatment of Joachim with his flocks. The bringing of the glad tidings to the shepherds, shown in the right foreground, is a complete picture story in itself, and here is the traditional sureness of touch which we associate with Byzantine art. Mary lies in a depression in the rock, as in all the Byzantine Christmas scenes. The other figures, especially the women, are full of grace and finely drawn, and the draping of the garments suggests spirited movement. They have had a powerful influence on Christian art in the East. Recent researches have identified the benefactors portrayed in the medallions; among them are Theodorus Metochites and the sister of Andronicus II, which fixes the date of this most important and best-preserved work of the Palaeologan renaissance somewhere between 1307 and 1320.

The Nativity. Mosaic. 1307–20. Kariye Cami, Constantinople (Istanbul)

Cattolica (catholicon), Stilo, Calabria. Domed cruciform church. Thirteenth century

The domed cruciform church was the building which had the greatest effect on neighboring countries, and indeed, as far as the outer edges of the Byzantine Empire. It endured even when direct contact with Constantinople was no longer maintained. In Greece, this type was usually given corner domes and a proportionately higher central one, an arrangement particularly favored for smaller buildings. Russian architects readily adapted the plan, a circumstance which may have stemmed from the presence in Russia of a large number of Greek master builders during the twelfth century. Many of their churches are on a square plan with an extension into one or three apses on one side only.

The South Italian churches which interest us here are two smaller ones of the more or less standard type, the *Cattolica* at Stilo, Calabria, and that of Saint Mark in Rossano, Calabria. Such churches of the thirteenth century have little in common with the monumental churches created in Sicily by the Normans; they are an outstanding example of the establishment of the smaller Byzantine five-domed type in a land outside the Empire. The central dome covers the space over four great piers standing in a square; from the outside, all the domes are smooth and unpretentious cylinders with almost conical roofs.

The last dynasty of the Palaeologi, which in the person of Michael VIII (1259–83) produced a ruler capable of restoring the waning power of the Empire, left in the capital only a few traces of memorable buildings. The craftsmen appear to have been satisfied with what came to hand and merely to have added more or less superfluous embellishments to existing plans. At the same period, however, Salonika was at the center of a quite astonishing resurgence of interest in church building, and among the great achievements, the Church of the Holy Apostles is outstanding. It was founded in 1312–13 by the Patriarch Niphon of Constantinople, who was of Macedonian origin, to serve as the church of a Theotokos (Mother of God) monastery. The external walls form an almost perfect square. The central dome and the four auxiliary domes build up impressively to a climax, forming a lively group over the basic square and repeating precisely the articulation of the interior. The shrine at the core of the building is small but lofty, a square with three apses, in the center of which four piers rise up to support the high dome above. It is surrounded on three sides by an ambulatory and has cupolas over the four corners. A wide outer narthex extends beyond the portal and its front is ornamented with arcades. As is quite usual in Salonika, external decoration depends largely on ingenious arrangements of ornamental brickwork.

Church of the Holy Apostles, Salonika. 1312–15

Monastery of Saint Paul. Probably founded in the tenth century. Mount Athos, Greece

As early as the ninth century, groups of monks and hermits were already established on Athos when it was scarcely yet a settled region. The development of the Holy Mountain of the monks dates, strictly speaking, from the coming of Saint Athanasius who founded the Great Lavra monastery here in 963, which in 971 received solemn recognition from the Emperor John I Zimiskes (969–76) forming the basis of the exceptional political privileges the monks enjoyed here. Monastic life reached its finest flowering in the thirteenth and fourteenth centuries. It was during this period that the Serbian ruler, Stephen Dushan, gave the Serbian foundations on Mount Athos particular support, among them the famous Chilandari monastery.

Turbulent rivers, swollen by waters that gather in the mountains, intersect the peninsula, on which the monasteries are situated like forbidding citadels. The monastery of Saint Paul is attributed to a legendary founder of the time of Saint Athanasius. In the fourteenth century, it passed into the possession of the Serbian monks and was not restored to the Greeks until the nineteenth century.

The heart of a monastery is its *catholicon* (monastic church), and as good an example as any is that in the Great Lavra, so firmly associated with the name of Saint Athanasius. We are told that, when he tried to save the structure of the dome in 1004, he was killed by the collapse of part of the vaulting. The catholicon is a domed cruciform church within a square with three apses, which had a liturgical significance in the monastic services and their choral chant. The illustration shows the octagonal main apse and one of the semicircular side apses. A nave is almost entirely lacking, for there is no question of accommodating laymen in the church. Athanasius had forbidden access to the Holy Mountain for "women and those without beards." The monks devoted their lives to asceticism, to meditation, and to art. It was particularly from the time of the Palaeologi onward that they took up the painting of icons.

Catholicon of the Great Lavra monastery. Founded 960. Mount Athos, Greece

THE SPREAD OF BYZANTINE ART IN THE EAST:
SERBIA, MACEDONIA, AND ROMANIA

Under the Palaeologi, the painting of panels and plaques (as distinguished from immovable murals) received such a vigorous impetus that examples were to be found wherever the influence of Byzantium reached. Up to a point, this new demand for portable icons was a result of the introduction of the *iconostasis* into churches, the two-part screen separating chancel from nave and designed to be covered with icons. Another spur was the readiness of merchants to buy icons for export. In Ohrid and on Mount Athos, imported icons in considerable numbers have been identified.

The photographs reproduced here are deceptive as to the true size of the icons. The upper level of the *iconostasis,* where the patron saints' icons were, often carried figures of more than life-size.

Icon of the Archangel Michael (detail). Tempera. Fourteenth century. Byzantine Museum, Athens

Christic as Saviour of Souls. Byzantine icon. Tempera, linen on wood, in silver setting, $36^1/_4 \times 26^1/_2''$. Beginning of fourteenth century. National Museum, Ohrid, Yugoslavia

The Annunciation. Reverse side of an icon of *Mary, Saviour of Souls.* Tempera, linen on wood, 36¹/₄ × 26³/₄″. Beginning of fourteenth century. National Museum, Ohrid, Yugoslavia

The icons of Ohrid play a major role in the later development of Serbian icon painting. It is not easy to discover links with the various schools of painting, the more especially as Serbian icons usually bear Greek inscriptions. There are two important icons in Ohrid which date from the beginning of the fourteenth century and which are a landmark in the history of Serbian art. They represent Christ and Mary as Saviours of Souls. Not only the type but the actual icons were probably imported from Byzantium. Andronicus II Palaeologus in the early fourteenth century presented the monastery of the Mother of God, Saviour of Souls, in Constantinople to Archbishop Gregory of Ohrid who appointed a monk of Ohrid as abbot. Thus it is very probable that the latter presented these icons from his Constantinople monastery to the cathedral in Ohrid.

The reverse side of the icon of Mary shows an *Annunciation,* one of the finest works of the early Palaeologan period. The beautifully worked-out proportions between the majestic architectural features in the background and the figures before them, the contrapuntal harmony between the rapidly approaching angel and the Madonna serene and motionless, the play of light and shadow, and the radiant color of the various objects in the scene made it a precious source of inspiration for later Serbian painters.

The Virgin Mary. Detail of illustration on facing page

After the fall of Constantinople, the Balkan lands were able to detach themselves politically, but in the sphere of art Byzantium was still the great example for them and the model on which they sought to base their own structures of state. This was the period in which the Serbian Empire leaped into prominence. Stephen II first had himself crowned king by a papal emissary in 1217, but he promptly set about demonstrating his independence of Rome by trading largely with Byzantium and by founding, with his brother, Saint Sava, an autonomous archiepiscopal province. He then had himself crowned again, by Saint Sava, this time with the Orthodox rite. In the reign of his successor Stephen Uros Miljutin (1282–1321), Serbia became a powerful Balkan state. Miljutin, through his first marriage with a Byzantine princess—both his first and his second wives were of the imperial house—and through his political aspirations, was still closely allied to Byzantium. Then northern Macedonia came under his sway. The zeal for building which affected most of the aristocratic families was a reflection of the growing cohesion and authority of the state, but the architectural concepts and the decoration alike were purely Byzantine.

The building of the church of the Mother of God at Studenica at the end of the twelfth century was commissioned by Stephen Nemanja (1190–1200), founder of the great Serbian ruling house. In its basic form and architectural adjuncts it is very much in the Roman tradition. The single-aisled, vaulted church with three apses culminates in a square section topped by a lofty dome which the Byzantine architect faced with bricks taken from Roman ruins. The original building was generously faced with marble and was throughout of the highest technical standard, under fifty feet long, and designed from the very beginning to serve eventually as the royal mausoleum. Instead of the transverse arm of the cruciform plan, the church has two side porches. The principal entrance was at the west end, where it is now hidden by a spacious vestibule added in the thirteenth century.

The exceptionally elaborate portal reminds one of Lombard work and can scarcely have been that of local craftsmen. Its design follows that of early South Italian portals which were created by Western artists in an area of Byzantine influence. The tympanum shows Mary with the Christ Child between Gabriel and Michael. In the illustration below, the Child is missing from Mary's lap; this part of the sculpture had been lost but was recently discovered in rubble near the church and has now been replaced.

This type of high, narrow memorial church culminating in a dome comparable to a Western crossing tower and showing Western influence and romanesque forms lasted through into the fourteenth century. The painting and other interior decorations, however, still closely followed Byzantine precedents with only a few trivial deviations. The frescoes of the Studenica church date from 1206.

◀ Church of the Mother of God. c. 1196. Studenica, Yugoslavia

Madonna and Child with Angels. Tympanum. c. 1220. Church of the Mother of God, Studenica, Yugoslavia

Frieze of Angels (detail). Chancel wall painting. Mid-eleventh century. Saint Sophia, Ohrid

Whereas Byzantine churches depended almost entirely on mosaics for decoration, churches in the Balkans were almost exclusively decorated with wall paintings. The beginnings of Yugoslav-Serbian fresco art are to be sought in northern Macedonia, which had again come under Byzantine rule after the victory over the Bulgars in 1018. Constantinople established an independent Bulgarian archbishopric in Ohrid, to which a church of Saint Sophia belonged. Its frescoes were painted in the first half of the eleventh century and clearly show that the archdiocese's ecclesiastical self-sufficiency was something of an illusion. The incumbent, Archbishop Leo (1037–56), was Vicar-General of the Patriarchate of Hagia Sophia at Constantinople. He decided the themes of the paintings, which were expressly directed against the Church of Rome. Thus, in the chancel, there are thirteen patriarchs of Hagia Sophia, with whom the Bulgarian patriarch was associated as a representative of Eastern Christianity.

Frescoes in the middle of the chancel are very well preserved, since they were protected by a layer of white

Angel of the Annunciation. Wall painting from triumphal arch. End of twelfth century. Church of Saint George, Kurbinovo

distemper until 1955. They are calm and lucid in style with the folds of the robes clearly marked. The emphatic fresco style has much in common with contemporary Byzantine mosaics, and it lasted right through the twelfth century. It had its greatest expression in Nerezi on Lake Prespa in northwestern Macedonia.

Kurbinovo also stands on Lake Prespa and, in the church of Saint George there, the northern Macedonian style is developed to the point of affectation. An inscription settles the date at 1191, so these paintings are contemporary with the chief mosaics of Saint Mark's in Venice. They represent the style of Byzantine provincial painting which was especially cultivated in Macedonia and, before long, even developed its own humor.

As the thirteenth century proceeded, there came into being, side by side with the fading northern Macedonian school of painting, a very different and original Serbian school. It may be said to have been in bud when the church of Mileševa, Yugoslavia, was decorated, and to have flowered in the frescoes of the monastery church of Sopoćani, also in Yugoslavia. The ambitious iconographic program of this royal foundation has several innovations which were to become part of the Serbian artists' range of themes. It is here in the north in particular that attempts are again made to convey the majesty as well as the mere configuration of these great figures. The slightly later (1295) frescoes of Saint Clement in Ohrid used the same themes but with some stiffness and affectation in the drapery while retaining a certain degree of bodily realism. This indicates

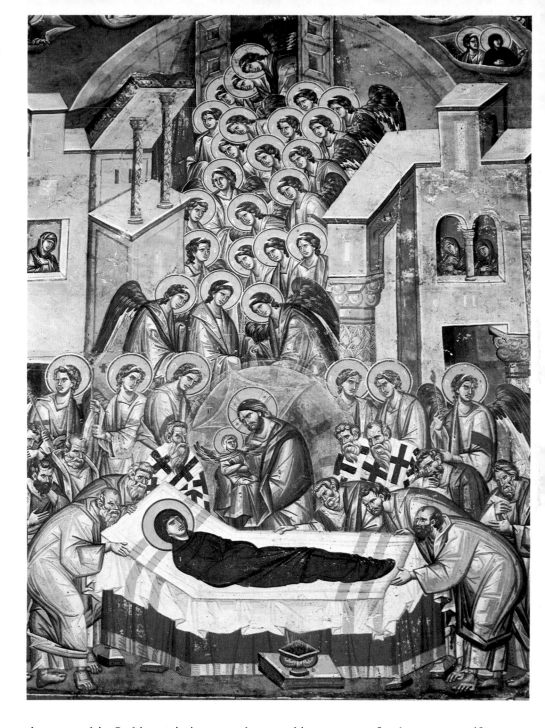

Mourning Apostle. Detail of wall painting of *Dormition of the Virgin.* c. 1265. Monastery church, Sopočani, Yugoslavia

Dormition of the Virgin. Wall painting. c. 1295. Church of Saint Clement, formerly Saint Mary Peribleptos, Ohrid, Yugoslavia

that the individuality we have noted in Serbian painting must be an achievement confined to one specific group or school and cannot readily be assumed to have become general in the region of Macedonia. It is significant that this church was commissioned by a Byzantine patron, and we know the names of the painters —Michael Astrapas and Eutychius—who were probably Greeks.

Birth of the Virgin. 1314. Royal church of Saints Joachim and Anne, Studenica, Yugoslavia

The further development of the Serbian school of painters is associated with the name of King Miljutin. In 1314, he had the royal church of Studenica built and decorated by his own painters. These were undoubtedly from the same school as the artists of Saint Clement, Ohrid. Michael Astrapas and Eutychius became court painters to Miljutin and their style is not far removed from that of Byzantine painters of Palaeologan times. Formal structure absorbs them; so does the use of space. In the church in Studenica dedicated by King Miljutin to Saints Joachim and Anne, the parents of the Virgin Mary, architectural features and a continuous series of events from the life of the young Virgin are harmoniously combined, each episode being framed

within a separate zone. The architecture and the figures are indeed so well combined that the figures actually depend on the architecture in making certain aspects of them clear. This reminds us that the paintings are of the same date as Giotto's "architectural" pieces at Assisi and Padua. Here in this little church we find the highest achievement of the Serbian painters.

The much larger church at Gračanica, Yugoslavia, one of the key buildings of medieval Serbia, offered vast areas of wall to the painters' brushes. Thus it is here that we have one of the outstanding groups of Serbian frescoes which, unlike the Studenica paintings, reveals the dark side of the elements which the artists chose to borrow from the Byzantium of the Palaeologi. The monumental figures we have met in Ohrid and Sopočani are transmuted: they are themselves more animated in their movements, but at the same time the inner rhythm of their proportions and the folds of their robes have stiffened.

Instead of disciplined and clear-cut composition, the artists have chosen to multiply themes and their iconography is far from being traditional. The canonical representation of the Dormition of the Virgin is combined with the bearing away of the dead body by the Apostles and yields to the resulting compulsion to introduce more movement with the figures. The nimbus around Christ, who carries off Mary's soul, forms a complicated, multipartite design. Similarly, the artist goes astray in his failure to exploit his wall space to best advantage; he uses the huge wall areas for a profuse number of pictures which have no place in a monumental composition but which are more like a series of individual icons painted on the wall.

Church of the Annunciation, Gračanica, Yugoslavia. c. 1320

The architecture of Gračanica is much like that of the capital in Palaeologan times—one might even coin the phrase "Palaeologan baroque" to describe it. This Serbian church seems to justify the description. King Miljutin built it in about 1320 as the cathedral of the bishopric of Sipljan. The ground plan is the familiar cross

within a square and the three apses do not extend far beyond the quadrilateral within which all the complications of the interior plan are concentrated, so that these express themselves only in the pleasing interaction of vaults and roofs. Bands of red brick and masonry alternate, with white pointing adding to the decorative effect. The repetition of the arch motif in the gables through the roof contours creates an ever more concentrated upward movement rising to the domes.

The painters of Gračanica, of whom there must surely have been almost a school, used wide means of artistic expression. The illustration above introduces us to an artist whose Byzantine repertoire of forms has been deeply affected by early-fourteenth-century Western practice, but which is scarcely at all mannered in the way the *Dormition of the Virgin* fresco is. Elijah in the wilderness is a being apart, shut off by the enclosing walls of his cave, which follow the line of his head and body much like the outlines of a church roof rising from apse to dome. With these artists, the enclosing motif and the expressive content it embraces, as well as the connection between incident and architectonic or natural setting, bring Giotto's frescoes at Padua to mind again and again.

As there were so many themes for painters to choose from, it is obvious that many churches had no coherent overall scheme of decoration. This Paradise scene, with saints being ministered to by angels in a wide landscape bounded by a heavily battlemented wall, is simply another form of that art which aimed at meeting a given theme with as great a skill and appropriateness as possible. A comparison of the angels here with the one in the painting opposite makes it clear that they are both of the same date.

Paradise with Saints and Ministering Angels. Wall painting. c. 1320. Church of the Annunciation, Gračanica, Yugoslavia

The representation of the founder in the painting here corresponds to one of 1314 in Miljutin's Studenica church. The smooth fall of the ceremonial robes is in the Byzantine metropolitan tradition and the representation of the model of the church is in both cases typical. The outlines of the building are so realistic that there can be no question of mistaking its identity.

223

The Women at the Tomb. Wall painting. c. 1235. Mileševa, Yugoslavia

The Mileševa paintings of 1235 stand at the beginning of Serbian painting in Yugoslavia. Of course, they are also Byzantine, but they reflect more the art of Western Europe as influenced directly by Constantinople. The angel in the painting of *The Women at the Tomb* shows archaic elements such as we recognize from Italian art in the thirteenth century. The firmly rounded, three-dimensional style of this painting has found new, and perhaps even more classical, form of expression in the Sopočani frescoes.

At approximately the same time the frescoes in the small funerary chapel of Boïana, Bulgaria, were painted. They were rediscovered in 1919 and at that time, when little was known about Serbian art, they created a sensation. Even today when the first glow of delight over them has faded in comparison with the Serbian frescoes of Mileševa and Sopočani, it must not be forgotten that they are a unique achievement at such an almost unbelievably early date. The profoundly psychological approach, the arrangement of draperies which contrive to be both realistic and ornamental without losing rhythm and meaning, the dark blue of the ground, the airy spaciousness of the canopy, the technique of applying the tempera color—all these are

aspects that one would expect to find in the fourteenth rather than the thirteenth century. But the frescoes have an inscription which settles their date. One fact is clear; they stand alone in a realm in which there is still a yawning chasm between early efforts and the later results that led from them. We still have much to learn about the course of developments in Bulgarian art, which differed so sharply from that of neighboring Serbia.

Monastery church, Voronezh, Romania. 1488–1547

Churches with frescoes on exterior walls were typical in Romania. Mostly we are concerned with buildings of the fifteenth century, the interiors of which were adorned with paintings almost as soon as they were built. As for the paintings on the outside walls, it was usually assumed that they were more or less contemporary: recent study has shown that quite a large proportion of them, at least, are of the sixteenth century.

They represent a quite unique and original use of painting, and with it, architecture. The monastery church of Voronezh glows like a jewel box in the landscape, and we tend to overlook its dimensions which are only ninety feet by thirty-six. The frescoes which completely cover the walls are all part of an integrated program, a homogeneous work of art with no later additions. They completely master and utilize architecture which was never conceived specifically for them, but to the surfaces of which they mold themselves so fittingly. Only the large unbroken surface of the west front was obviously intended for painting, as we know from the church's building history.

The monastery was founded during the reign of Stephen the Great (1457–1504) and the dedicatory inscription associates it with his victory over the Turks. The first church on the site was somewhat smaller than the present one and the outside was decorated with colored glass bricks. Under Peter Rares (1527–38), it was customary to have enclosed forecourts in front of churches and all the external walls painted. Apparently the practice of having the entrances at the sides of the church, toward the west end, was connected with the need to allow a large unbroken surface on the west for painting. At Voronezh, the narthex was built after the completion of the external frescoes everywhere else. The great *Last Judgment* (below) also belongs to the end of the rebuilding period in 1550. High above are angels pulling away the shrouds of Time and in the middle is the figure of God the Father. Below is the Glorification of Jesus, who stands with the Apostles, Mary, and Saint John, presented here as an extensive *Deesis* (picture of the Virgin Mary enthroned between the Apostles and Saint John). In the third zone from the top is the Apocalyptic theme of the "Hetoimasia," the preparation of the Throne. Here the righteous and the unrighteous are separated and below rages the battle between angels and devils for the possession of souls.

Monastery church, Voronezh, Romania. West front

◀ Monastery church, Voronezh. Side apse

The Blessed Virgin and the Christ Child Ringed by Angels. Dome fresco. 1488–1547. Monastery church, Voronezh, Romania

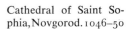

Maria Orans above the ▶ *Communion of the Apostles.* Apse mosaic. c. 1050. Saint Sophia, Kiev

RUSSIAN ART

The people of Kiev in Russia had accepted Christianity from Bulgarian missionaries in the tenth century and they came closer to the Byzantine world again when Prince Vladimir married Princess Anna, sister of the Byzantine Emperor Basil II, in 989. He certainly brought craftsmen from Byzantium to build his Koimesis church in 996. Excavations on the site of the vanished church have shown that it had a domed cruciform plan, based on the Greek cross, as did the church at neighboring Chernigov, built for Yaroslav the Wise, who also began the Saint Sophia of Kiev. This latter church was certainly modeled on the Hagia Sophia in Constantinople, but for all that, it yields so much evidence of originality that it cannot be satisfactorily classified. Rebuilding has since changed it almost beyond recognition.

The basic plan is known to us through the simpler form preserved in Saint Sophia, Novgorod, founded in 1050 by Yaroslav's son Vladimir. Instead of thirteen domes, there are a mere seven, since there are only three aisles to be covered. This church was built by Vladimir to replace his grandfather's foundation and is of timber construction typical of northern Russia. Novgorod now distinguished itself from Kiev by the pronounced tendency toward vertical lines which came to typify the Russian style for sacred edifices, though these show a renewed inclination toward the domed cruciform plan.

Christ Pantocrator Surrounded by Angels. Dome mosaic. c. 1050. Saint Sophia, Kiev

Like his father Vladimir I, Yaroslav brought in "artists from the land of the Greeks" to adorn his Saint Sophia in Kiev, begun in 1037. The only mosaic decoration here is in the apse, there being frescoes everywhere else. In the dome is a huge, majestic Pantocrator surrounded by four angels; the Apostles appear below with Evangelists and martyrs. In the apse mosaic, the Virgin in the *orant* attitude of prayer has an expanse of gold behind her (page 231). At a lower level and in one broad band a most unusual scene is depicted, one which a little later will be seen among the sumptuous mosaics of Kiev's Saint Michael's church. This is the *Communion of the Apostles.* It had a Byzantine origin and is a symbolic allusion to the institution of the sacrament of Holy Communion. On both sides of the altar, Christ is seen administering the sacramental bread

Communion of the Apostles. Apse mosaic. c. 1050. Saint Sophia, Kiev

and wine. The two figures on the extreme edges of the scene are Aaron and Melchizedek, who prefigured in their sacrifices in the Old Testament the eucharistic sacrifice of Christ in the New. The mosaics resemble, stylistically, those of Nea Moni on the island of Chios and those of Daphni, but are distinguished from these by a somewhat outmoded emphasis in the outlines and by the massive bulk of the figures. There is a very rich gradation of color here—over a hundred tones and shades have been counted. Most of the mosaic pieces are of glass paste made in workshops on the spot, as excavations have proved. No doubt Byzantine artists brought with them the few tools they required.

More recent Russian research indicates that some of the Saint Sophia mosaics in Kiev were made by native Russian artists and craftsmen. This seems to be the case particularly with the figures of saints around the apse. This assumption is strongly supported by the fact that three other contemporary churches in Kiev had mosaic adornments, so that quite a large band of artists would have been employed. All these mosaics show a distinct liking for an overall pale pink tone, also characteristic of enamels which were undoubtedly the work of Russians. In certain types of head, some have claimed to see purely Russian features; the Kiev mosaics

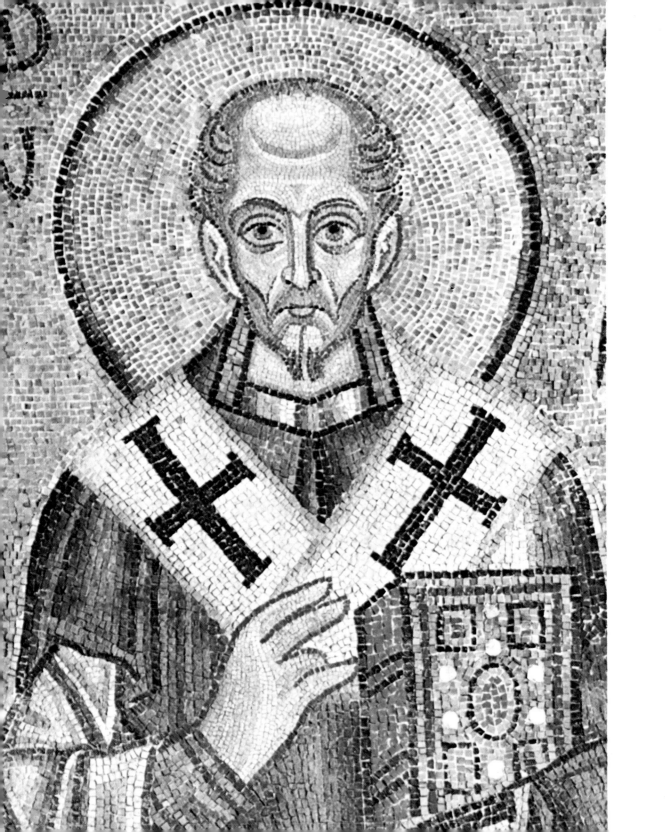

◀ *Saint Nicholas*. Mosaic. Mid-eleventh century. Saint Sophia, Kiev

The Visitation of Mary. Wall painting in the Chapel of Saints Joachim and Anne. Mid-eleventh century. Saint Sophia, Kiev

certainly all have much in common and are distinguished from Byzantine mosaics of the lands bordering the Mediterranean, which at this time were experiencing a decline before the urban art of fresco painting.

Its design and basic plan make Kiev's Saint Sophia one of the most subtly and beautifully proportioned buildings of the West in the early Middle Ages. Because of its extraordinary size, it could not be decorated throughout with mosaics and was therefore one of the first Russian churches to use paintings on a large scale. The painters leaned heavily on Byzantine models, and where they seem to have had no knowledge of these, they made imaginative attempts to simulate the great models of the South that they admired so much. One individual trait of the Russians, one with no Byzantine forerunner, is the blending of painting and mosaic in one decorative scheme. The frescoes of Saint Sophia in Kiev form a continuous cycle which could not have been successfully interpreted in any other way. The great stories of sacred history are narrated in a colorful sequence arranged according to the canons of Byzantine art. But the saints' cycles in the side chapels deviate from them, concentrating on events in the life of the titular saint of each one. The decoration in the chapel dedicated to Saints Joachim and Anne includes many episodes in the life of the Virgin. The architectural backgrounds are simple, boldly outlined, almost flat, and the figures are treated in a simplified, almost summary way with the emphasis on gesture.

The date of these frescoes is known fairly closely. In the center of the east wall there is a founder's portrait showing Yaroslav and his family handing over the model of the church. Four of his five daughters stand in line carrying tapers, the figure of the eldest daughter having been eliminated later. This was done in 1044 or 1045, when she was twenty years old and had married the King of Norway. The second daughter, who looks about seventeen years old as she stands in the row, later married the King of France, dating the fresco at about 1045. It also shows how close the links were binding the Western courts and the young Russian state which dealt with them on equal terms, a relationship which was bound to be reflected before long in Russian art.

Yaroslav's court artists took full advantage of the five aisles of the Saint Sophia cathedral, and even the lateral bays were lavishly adorned with paintings. All these works were painted over in oils in the nineteenth century, so that their original state is scarcely to be recognized today. Yaroslav was a firm supporter of the monastic and feudal church. We read in a contemporary chronicle, "For Yaroslav cherished the precepts of the Church; he admired priests, but monks still more." When he had the Saint Sophia cathedral built, he was hoping thereby to affirm that Russia had been saved from "heathen darkness" through the light of holy wisdom, associating this happy deliverance with his own position as Grand Duke and representative of the authority of the state, just as was the case in Byzantium. A strange sequence of pictures illustrates this.

In the two towers with staircases that served members of the grand-ducal court as a means of access to the galleries, the walls are painted with circus scenes. Actors

Audience at a Circus. Wall painting on staircase. Mid-eleventh century. Saint Sophia, Kiev ▶

Wall paintings in aisle. Mid-eleventh century. Saint Sophia, Kiev wage mock battles in animal disguises and musicians accompany the performances. There is also the common motif of a bear fighting a lion; it is as though we were witnessing here a merry sequence of human pleasures as opposed to the world of the religious images in the church interior. Many such pictures become comprehensible enough when we read, in the chronicles of the time, how passionately Yaroslav was addicted to games, spectacles, and hunting, even being reproached for his tastes. Both towers have pictures including the great rostrum with the ruler presiding over the circus. We know the theme from Byzantine imperial ceremonial, a theme inherited from Rome and from the consular and imperial diptychs. Since Justinian's day, presiding at the circus had been one of the imperial public functions. By the middle of the tenth century, the Christianization of "Rus" centered on Kiev had begun. A century later the Russian grand duke was as powerful within his dominions as the ruler of Byzantium was in his own. His daughters were marrying great European monarchs and Russian art was so distinguished in its own right that it could now assimilate all kinds of alien influences and fuse them into new styles without losing its individuality. From now onward, these influences worked on North Russian art in Vladimir-Suzdal, and Novgorod farther north, for the Mongol conquests of the twelfth century brought Kiev's supremacy to an end.

The Spasa church, Novgorod. 1374

To the west and east of Moscow, the future capital, two powerful communities which quite clearly differed from one another had developed. Vladimir-Suzdal was closely associated with, and took much inspiration from, Kiev; Novgorod was, in keeping with its origins, a community of traders and artisans. Its political structure showed parallels with city-states in the West, and its monasteries were much more comparable with Western foundations, being centers of settlement and colonization, large-scale entrepreneurs (which their far-reaching feudal supremacy made possible), and providers of development aid in the form of new agricultural methods. In those days, the way of life in the Russian north was sober, down-to-earth, and open to new influences. The architecture, too, was simple and solid, with frequent echoes of Western Imperial styles.

In 1045, the son of Grand Duke Vladimir of Kiev decreed that Saint Sophia should be built in Novgorod. Soon after it came into being he withdrew his grand-ducal rights and entrusted its charge to the bishop. At the same time, Novgorod was developing its own style in art, which found its finest expression in the Cathedral of the Transfiguration, built in 1189 on Nereditsa Hill. This was utterly destroyed during the last war. With the Mongol invasions of the thirteenth century, as well as the attacks of Germans, Swedes, and Lithuanians, there came a period of setbacks which were only overcome in the fourteenth century. During these years, Novgorod evolved an architectural style entirely its own, building small square churches with sloping roofs and a high central tower holding aloft the dome.

All such churches had their external wall surfaces whitened and marked off into separate areas with bands in relief. The applied ornament shown on the walls of the church illustrated on the facing page goes beyond architectural practice common in Novgorod. The Spasa church was erected by the citizens of Ilya Street and it shows the typical Novgorod style of the fourteenth century. Churches of this kind were particularly suitable as places of worship for exclusive groups of citizens, for guilds and similar bodies. It was not a type that was evolved independently; it was based on the smaller type of Greek church, but modified in a particular way in Vladimir-Suzdal in the years when the Grand Duke Andrei Boguljubski (1157–74) was bringing the principality of Vladimir to its greatest period. He brought in Western craftsmen and architects who combined Western architectural practice with Byzantine forms, so that these took on a typically romanesque aspect, detectable in the layout of the city of Vladimir as well. Church authority had a characteristically Russian aspect there, however, and resisted Byzantine influence from Kiev. Against the wishes of the ecclesiastical authorities in Kiev, the new Feast of *Pokrov* (Mary of Refuge) was instituted in Vladimir. As an

"architectonic forecourt to his city of residence, Boguljubi," Andrei Boguljubski had a monastery, dedicated to Mary of Refuge, built on the River Nerl' where ships coming to his principality had their moorings. The airy proportions of his church with its elegant vertical lines and the superb masons' work later to be hidden under whitewash make their full effect in this building's isolated position today. If we compare it with the later church at Novgorod, both the resemblances and the further development that this type of building underwent are quite apparent.

Church of Mary of Refuge, Bogolyoboro, near Vladimir. 1165

The wars with the Mongols resulted in the emergence of Moscow to a position of importance in the four-teenth century, and soon the city became a Russian political and cultural center. Here the architectural styles for churches developed in Vladimir-Suzdal were at first adopted: the square plan with four piers at the core and three apses. Then Ivan III (1462–1505) made his own principality the strongest in the Russian terri-tories and at once sealed his success by undertaking an ambitious building program. He brought not only the best Russian architects, but also Italian ones, to Moscow. The Bolognese Rodolfo Fioravanti was commis-sioned to build the Koimesis cathedral in the Kremlin in the years between 1475 and 1479. It was to be rooted in Russian tradition and Fioravanti was instructed to contribute his technical skills rather than his artistic concepts; thus he was sent to Vladimir to study the church of the Assumption there and to learn from it the basic elements of the Russian tradition. He had, in fact, to conform to the architecture of the end of the twelfth century, but by making certain adjustments in the proportions, and by relating them to one another

Koimesis cathe-dral, Kremlin, Moscow. 1475–79

Cathedral of the
Annunciation,
Kremlin, Mos-
cow. 1482–90

in the way that was being done in Italian architecture of the fifteenth century, Fioravanti achieved a variation in his fairly narrowly prescribed models which has particularly harmonious lines to eyes schooled in the Western architectural tradition. The three-aisled church with its five domes is shown here from the south.

From 1482 to 1490, Ivan III's baptistery church, the cathedral of the Annunciation, was erected at his palace. This time Ivan summoned builders from Pskov because of their well-known technical capabilities. Here again, it was a matter of a rebuilding which Ivan did not entrust to builders from Moscow because he wished to avoid the unfortunate experiences he had had with them in the course of earlier projects before Rodolfo Fioravanti was summoned to work on the cathedral. Pskov lay to the west of Novgorod and was reputed to be a city exceptionally zealous and experienced in building. The cathedral of the Annunciation, unlike contemporary Moscow buildings obviously the work of the Pskov masters, shows no traces of their individual style. They did, however, apply an entirely new method to the building of the dome, omitting the interior supporting piers, so that it now rested on an ingenious system of staggered, forward-projecting vaults. This technique, which also made a difference to the outside appearance of the dome, became characteristic of Moscow churches until well into the seventeenth century. It entails a staggering of the roof vaulting up as far as the central dome, so that this becomes almost a continuation of it.

The Kremlin on its triangular hillside between Moskva and Neglinnaya, with its palaces and churches behind long walls, gives a panoramic view of the achievements of Russian architecture. Italian architects, in particular Fioravanti, Pietro Solari, and Marco Ruffo, set up the strong walls and towers, and in 1542 Marco Bono completed his great bell tower, the "Ivan Veliki," which introduced Italian tower building to Moscow. In 1505, Aleviso Novi built the cathedral of the Archangels, which combines Russian architecture with Renaissance ornamentation.

From the reign of Ivan the Terrible (1533–84), rich in extravagance, dates the oddest of churches, Saint Basil. Its architects, Postnik and Barma, were instructed to group eight free-standing chapels around a central one dedicated to Our Lady of Refuge. Later on, the form of the church was altered, and today it has the appearance of a building of the end of the seventeenth century. It is to this church that the legend is attached that Ivan the Terrible had both architects blinded, so that they could never repeat their achievement for anybody else.

Great bell tower, Kremlin, Moscow. 1542

Church of Saint Basil (formerly cathedral of the Intercession), Moscow. 1555–60, with seventeenth-century additions

Christ Pantocrator with Angels. Dome painting by Theophanes the Greek. c. 1370. Cathedral of the Transfiguration, Novgorod

In the fourteenth century, several Russian painters of outstanding talent came to the fore: they are to be recognized by their personal styles, as with artists of the Trecento in Italy. These Russian painters were also traditionalists. The first great figure towered above all others in Novgorod: Feofan Grek, or Theophanes the Greek, a member of the Constantinople school of painters. He left the capital either because of its decline or because of the strife over the Hesychasts (an ascetic sect of mystics from Mount Athos). His wider activity is well documented, for he painted in Chalcedon (Kadiköy), Galati, and Kaffa before working as a manuscript

Prophet. School of Theophanes the Greek. c. 1378. Cathedral of the Transfiguration, Novgorod

illuminator and icon painter in Novgorod where he also decorated "probably more than forty" stone churches (to quote a document of the time). He went on to Moscow and there painted the interiors of three churches, distinguishing himself as a versatile and accomplished artist; for instance, he painted a panorama of the whole of Moscow on a wall for a certain prince, and for a supplicant he painted a picture of Hagia Sophia in Constantinople. His memory for details of form was marvelous, enabling him to paint without always having precedents to follow. In Moscow he worked with the foremost Russian artist of the Middle Ages, the monk Andrei Rublyov.

Surviving Novgorod paintings by Theophanes are quite different from what we know of Greek painting of the fourteenth century. Out of the stage of development reached in the Kariye Cami paintings, Theophanes' encounters with the Novgorod School and that North Russian city's intellectual freedom enabled him to evolve a new style which was of fundamental importance for Russian painting of the fifteenth century.

Icon of the Trinity. Tempera on wood by Andrei Rublyov, 55⅞ × 44⅞″. c. 1411. Tretiakov Gallery, Moscow

Mantle of the Madonna. Wall painting by the master Denys. c. 1500. Monastery, Therapon (Ferapont)

Theophanes the Greek arrived in Moscow when Russian painting was at its height with two important Russian masters at work. At the beginning of the century he met the monk Andrei Rublyov in Moscow who shared a workshop with an older artist, Daniel Tschornizh. Rublyov's chief work is the Holy Trinity icon representing the Trinity of the Old Testament in the form of the three angels who were with Abraham. He painted it in memory of his abbot and patron Saint Sergius of Radonezh, who died in 1411. Rublyov entered a monastery at an early age and was already a monk when he became assistant to Theophanes in 1405. He was primarily an icon painter at a time when the decoration of churches was being centered more and more on the iconostasis, the wall of icons separating the chancel from the rest of the church. The flat lyrical style and the harmonious tranquillity of the Holy Trinity icon led to such a great veneration for his work that he was finally canonized. This icon is the only one that can now be definitely attributed to him.

In the second half of the fifteenth century, the icon painter Denys carried on Rublyov's tradition, but he dissolved the harmony of Rublyov's surfaces, deploying his figures in spatial units defined by pieces of stagelike scenery. At the same time, a certain stylization and stiffness can be traced in his work. The frescoes in the Therapon (Russian Ferapont) monastery show him freed from the constraints of the icon tradition and much more at ease in wider spaces. According to an inscription, the Ferapont frescoes were painted by Denys and his two sons between 1500 and 1502.

Saint George Slaying the Dragon.
Icon. Tempera on wood, $22\frac{7}{8}$ x $16\frac{1}{8}''$.
End of fourteenth century. Novgorod
School. Russian State Museum, Leningrad

The icons of Russia are among the most important of all medieval works of art, though for a long time they were admired only by a few specialists. Their artistic merit lies above all in their colors, but it is these which have been so long obscured. The icons are cult objects which have been kept for centuries in dark churches and, worst of all, have often been coated with thick brown varnish or with overpainting. Today the finest examples have been cleaned and freed from all later additions in the great Russian museums. Those which reached the West give only a meager idea of the splendor and the quality of this art.

Novgorod saw the beginnings of the art of icon painting in Russia. In the twelfth century, the icons of the "golden-haired archangel" were produced; he became typical thereafter for angels in icons. With the coming of the fifteenth century, Novgorod's leadership in this field was briefly usurped by Moscow's brilliant artists. At first, the Novgorod painters followed the Byzantine tradition closely; in the fourteenth century, however, an independent approach developed, local idiosyncracies were observable, and for both form and theme the icon artist no longer looked to Byzantium. The Novgorod painter liked his separate figures and objects to stand out clearly against a smooth, bright background. There is a particular preference for a vermilion ground which accentuates even more the foreground figures, and for an easily comprehended subject with clear outlines. The vividness of color should not be misunderstood as a primitive crudeness.

The theme we inevitably associate with the Novgorod school is that of Saint George and the Dragon, and also Elijah, "Voice of Thunder." But, above all, saints who had some connection with husbandry and livestock were preferred. Saint George thus figured as the protector of animals and Saints Laurus and Florus as patron saints of grooms and stablemen; for them the Novgorod artists used a style which recalls the noblest Persian miniatures of the time. Elijah was especially common as a protector against terrible fires and raging storms. In Novgorod, there were definite conventions for depicting saints, which later spread to other

centers. These types were even given names: "The Father's Lap" corresponded to something like the Western "Mercy Seat"; then there was a representation of the Mother of God called "Joy of All Creation," a "Mary of Refuge," and a "Christ with Fiery Eyes."

The Prophet Elijah. Icon. Tempera on wood, 29¹/₂ x 22¹/₂". c. 1400. Novgorod School. Tretiakov Gallery, Moscow

Icons could be single portable devotional objects or elements in an iconostasis. Starting with a Deesis, the iconostasis displayed, in the "feast rows," representations of the principal festivals of the Christian year. Then came the rows of icons of the prophets and Russian heroes. With the iconostasis separating the Holy of Holies from the congregation, the icon began replacing the fresco, taking over all the iconographic elements of the paintings on the walls.

Icon painting was considered the highest form of art in the Russia of the Middle Ages: to devote oneself to painting icons was to serve God. Notions of this kind may have been disseminated by the monastic communities of Mount Athos, and it is certainly true that some of the best icon painters were monks. The others lived in close contact with monks and bishops. The relationship between Saint Sergius of Radonezh and Andrei Rublyov has already been mentioned. So, in the *Stoglav*, an icon painter of the fourteenth century is described thus: "It is seemly for the painter to be meek and tender and orthodox in belief; above all, he must take every care to preserve spiritual and bodily purity . . . and it is seemly that the painter should come often to the holy fathers and take counsel with them over everything and live according to their precept and example. And the bishops should take great care, each in his diocese, to see that icon painters and their pupils paint according to the old styles and do not depict God after their own ideas and imaginings." These injunctions were strictly observed by the great masters of the fourteenth and fifteenth centuries. Denys came at a time when this tradition was dying, and he was followed by the mannerism of the sixteenth century which led to the debasement of the art of icon painting, the final fruit of Byzantine art.

Saints Florus and Laurus. Icon. Tempera on wood, 26 × 20½". Last quarter of fifteenth century. Novgorod School. Tretiakov Gallery, Moscow

Saint Sergius of Radonezh. Detail of an embroidered silk pall used to cover the tomb of the saint who was honored, as founder of the church of the Holy Trinity, by Rublyov with the Holy Trinity icon (page 247). The pall shows the saint lying full length on a blue ground and measures 77 x 32¹/₄″. It came almost certainly from the workshops of a grand-ducal court. Since Sergius was associated with the Moscow court as the tutor of princes and adviser, this portrait must have been produced at the time of the saint's death in the early years of the fifteenth century. Museum, Trinity–Saint Sergius Monastery, Zagorsk

Chronological Tables

CONSTANTINIAN AND THEODOSIAN AGE

260 Gallienus' Edict of Toleration grants Christians the right to possess their own churches.
Reforms of Diocletian and Constantine facilitate creation of state of Byzantium.
312 Battle of Milvian Bridge, after which Constantine declares Christianity the state religion.
324 Constantinople founded and entire administrative apparatus reorganized and removed to the new capital (330).
378 Roman forces (under Valens) routed by Goths at Adrianople.
379 Theodosius becomes ruler of Eastern Roman Empire; makes pact with Ostrogoths. Orthodox Christianity established as state religion.
395 Arcadius becomes ruler of Eastern Empire, recognizing it as more important half of the Empire.
476 Western Roman Empire comes to an end. Theodoric and Ostrogothic troops advance into Italy.
493 Bulgar invasions begin.

JUSTINIAN AND HIS TIME

527 Justinian becomes Emperor of Byzantium.
532 Suppression of Nika riots leads to reorganization of Empire.
Peace with Chosroes I (531–79), ruler of Persia.
540–72 Persian Wars.
568 Lombard invasions.
580 Slav invasions.
591 Peace with Chosroes II. Armenia conquered by Maurice (582–602).
Heraclius (610–41) repulses Avar and Persian attacks on Constantinople.
633–42 Islamic invasions in Syria, Mesopotamia, Palestine, and Egypt.
Successors of Heraclius extend his system of *themes* (division into military provinces) throughout the Empire.

ICONOCLASM

730 Leo III (717–41) enforces edict against display of images.
751 Exarchate of Ravenna abolished.
787 Council of Nicaea reverses Leo III's ban on images.
811 Bulgars defeat Byzantine forces.
827 Islamic invasions in Crete and Sicily.
843 End of iconoclasm.

864 Conversion of Bulgars to Christianity. Founding of Serbian state. Alliance between Novgorod and Kiev.

CLASSICISM AND DECLINE

Macedonian emperors (867–1056) send missions eastward in attempt to unite Latin and Greek churches.
963–69 Reconquest of Syria and Palestine.
988 Trade agreements with Russia lead to intensive program of Christianization in Russia, Bulgaria, Romania, and Serbia.
1014 West Bulgar Empire dissolved.
1071 Asia Minor relinquished.
Normans drive Byzantines from Italy.
1077 Jerusalem falls to Seljuk Turks.
1082 Alliances with and trading concessions for Venice in return for aid against Normans.
1185–1204 Angelus emperors of Byzantium suffer defeats.
1204 Conquest of Constantinople in Fourth Crusade. Disintegration of the Empire.
1223 Mongol invasions in Russia.
1258 Palaeologan dynasty tries in vain to restore the Empire. Ottoman Turks inflict permanent damage.
1331–55 Stephen Dushan rules in Serbia. Time of prosperity.
1380 Moscow becomes center of great Russian Empire. Its church frees itself from Byzantium.
1393 Bulgaria becomes Turkish province.
1444–48 Turks conquer Serbia. End of Serbian state.
1453 Constantinople falls to Mohammed II. Moscow takes over as leader of Orthodox Christianity.
After reign of Stephen the Great (1457–1504), Romania falls under Turkish domination.

CULTURAL HISTORY AND CHURCH HISTORY

CONSTANTINIAN AND THEODOSIAN AGE

Emperors retain title of *Pontifex Maximus* after Christianity has become state religion.
325 Ecumenical Council of Nicaea debates basic dogma of Christian church (establishment of creed).
State persecutes Arians.
351 Constantine encourages Arianism.
361 Julian reintroduces paganism.
364–78 Valens and Valentinian divide East and West into Arians and Orthodox.
381 Council of Constantinople outlaws Arianism.
425 Academy of Constantinople fostered and given key functions.

528 Tribonian codifies laws for Justinian as *Corpus Juris Civilis.*
529 Justinian closes pagan Academy of Athens.
550 *Topographia Christiana* of Cosmas Indicopleustes.
630 True Cross brought back to Constantinople.
The Empire becomes *imperium* of soldiers and monks.

ICONOCLASM

Popes Gregory II (715–31) and Gregory III (731–41) rule in the West.
727 In Jerusalem, John of Damascus expounds theology of icons in three *Homilies.*
Veneration replaces worship of images.
815 Reintroduction of iconoclasm. Shortly after, images set up again in Hagia Sophia.
Libri Carolini, Synod of Frankfurt (794), and Synod of Paris (825) show Western standpoint: opposition to both destruction and veneration of images, and emphasis on their instructional uses.

CLASSICISM AND DECLINE

829–976 "Macedonian Renaissance": return to Hellenistic ideals, with Photius (826–97) as outstanding advocate.
864 Mission of Cyril and Methodius to the Slavs.
913–59 Court ritual described in *Book of Ceremonies* as "the ornament and embellishment of the Empire."
Simeon Metaphrastes translates *Lives of the Saints* into rhetorical and literary language of his *Menologium.*
John Zimiskes (969–76) encourages spread of libraries and has books copied.
988 Missions to Russia.
1054 Final schism between Rome and Constantinople.
1081 Comnenus line of soldier-emperors interrupts cultural developments and discussion of Platonism.
After division of the Empire, landowners and merchants contribute most to furtherance of culture. Hellenistic past seen as spiritual ideal. Last ruler calls himself "King of the Hellenes."

ARCHITECTURE

CONSTANTINIAN AND THEODOSIAN AGE

313 San Giovanni in Laterano, Rome, begun.
323 Saint Peter's, Rome, begun.
335 First church of the Holy Sepulcher, Jerusalem.
360 Santa Maria Maggiore, Rome, begun.
386 San Paolo Fuori le Mura, Rome, begun.
391 Golden Gate, Constantinople.
400 Saint George, Salonika.
425–30 Santa Sabina, Rome.

after 450 Saint David, Salonika.
450–95 Both baptisteries in Ravenna.
c. 480 San Stefano Rotondo, Rome.

JUSTINIAN AND HIS TIME

c. 526 Mausoleum of Theodoric, Ravenna.
527–36 Great centrally planned churches of Constantinople: Saints Sergius and Bacchus, Hagia Sophia, Saint Irene.
547 Consecration of centrally planned church of San Vitale, Ravenna, alongside basilicas of Sant'Apollinare Nuovo and Sant'Apollinare in Classe.
625–38 Sant'Agnese Fuori le Mura, Rome.
634 Saint Demetrius, Salonika, rebuilt.
c. 750 Saint Irene, Constantinople, rebuilt.

ICONOCLASM

First half of 8th C. Palace of the Exarchs, Ravenna, built.
c. 850 Saint Sophia, Salonika, rebuilt.
c. 850 Koimesis church, Nicaea, built.

CLASSICISM AND DECLINE

c. 920–40 Myreleion monastery, Constantinople.
c. 960 Catholicon of Great Lavra monastery, Mount Athos.
c. 1000 Saint Sophia, Ohrid.
Early 11th C. Saint Luke of Stiris, Phocis.
1037–46 Saint Sophia, Kiev.
c. 1045 Nea Moni, Chios.
1046–50 Saint Sophia, Novgorod.
1042–71 Saint Mark's, Venice.
c. 1100 Monastery church, Daphni.
1130–52 Palermo and Cefalù.
1164 Panteleimon church, Nerezi.
1165 Church of Mary of Refuge, Bogolyoboro.
c. 1300 Rila monastery, Bulgaria.
c. 1400 Church of Mary Mother of God, Kalenić.
15th C. Kremlin, Moscow, rebuilt with help of Italian architects.

FIGURATIVE AND APPLIED ARTS

CONSTANTINIAN AND THEODOSIAN AGE

3rd C. Beginnings of Christian art during great period of Roman catacomb painting.
Mid-4th C. Tomb art reaches its peak:
c. 354 Porphyry sarcophagus of Constantia,
359 Sarcophagus of Junius Bassus.
c. 400 Enrichment of art through work of ivory carvers and other craftsmen:
c. 360 Brescia Lipsanotheca,

c. 400 Classical influence in diptych of Nicomachi and Symmachi,
c. 400 Miniatures of Ambrosian *Iliad,*
c. 430 Wooden door of Santa Sabina, Rome,
c. 500 Barberini ivory.
First half of 4th C. Mosaics of Santa Costanza, Rome, anticipate great mosaic decorations:
Late 4th C. Apse mosaic, Santa Pudenziana, Rome,
c. 400 Dome mosaic, Saint George, Salonika,
c. 425 Mausoleum of Galla Placidia, Ravenna,
432–40 Nave mosaic, Santa Maria Maggiore, Rome,
c. 458 Baptistery of the Orthodox, Ravenna.

JUSTINIAN AND HIS TIME

526 Mosaic work begun in great new Ravenna churches:
c. 540 Basilica Eufrasiana,
c. 547 San Vitale,
c. 549 Sant'Apollinare in Classe,
c. 560 Sant'Apollinare Nuovo.
546–56 Throne of Maximian, Ravenna.
560–70 Apse decoration of Sinai monastery, and mosaics in Panhagia Angeloktistos, Chiti.
c. 570 Paten from Riha.
c. 600 Monza *ampullae* from treasure of Theodolinda.
610–29 Nicosia silver dishes.
625–38 Apse mosaic, Sant'Agnese Fuori le Mura, Rome.

ICONOCLASM

Iconoclasm prevents practice and development of religious figurative art in the East.
Frescoes of Santa Maria Antica, Rome, completed.
Mid-8th C. Beginning of "Carolingian Renaissance" in Western Christian art.

CLASSICISM AND DECLINE

867–1056 "Macedonian Renaissance" grows out of iconoclast quarrels.
Mosaics:
Beginning of 11th C. Saint Luke of Stiris, Phocis,
1040–55 Nea Moni, Chios,
1056 Koimesis church, Nicaea,
c. 1100 Monastery church, Daphni.
Book illumination:
867–86 *Homilies of Gregory of Nazianzus,*
First half of 10th C. *Joshua Roll,*
c. 985 *Menologium of Basil II.*
Applied arts:
c. 940 Chalice of Romanus,
c. 965 Limburg Staurotheca,
10th–11th C. Veroli casket.
Mid-11th C. Frescoes in Saint Sophia, Kiev.
12th C. Period of great expansion of Byzantine art
In the West:
1129–43 Palatine chapel, Palermo,
1131–48 Cathedral, Cefalù,
1143–51 Martorana, Palermo,
After 1174 Basilica, Monreale,
Mosaics in Saint Mark's Venice, begun;
In the East:
1191 Saint George, Kurbinovo,
Frescoes in Vladimir-Suzdal,
Beginning of Russian icon painting,
c. 1295 Frescoes in Saint Clement, Ohrid,
1300–20 Mosaics in Kariye Cami, last great mosaic decoration in Constantinople,
Theophanes the Greek (1330–1410) and Andrei Rublyov (c. 1370–1430) mark the peak of Russian painting.

North Sea

Baltic Sea

Therapon

Novgorod

Pskov

Jaroslav

Tver   Suzdal   Nizhni Novgorod

Vladimir   Nerl'

Moscow   Bogolyoboro

Elbe   Oder

Polotsk

Rhine   Vistula

Smolensk

Chernigov

Volga

Danube   Sandomierz

Cracow   Galicia

Kiev

Suceava   Dniester   Dnieper   Don

Monza   Aquileia   Grado

Milan   Venice   Parenzo

Po

Ravenna   Gračanica

Curtea-de-Arges

Belgrade   Bucharest

Black Sea

Tiflis

Adriatic Sea

Mileševa   Kalenić

Sopoćani   Studenica   Sofia   Tirnovo   Sinop

Rome   Boïana   Trebizond

Monte Cassino   Monte Gargano   Ohrid   Nerezi   Constantinople   Chalcedon   Ahtamar

Barletta   Kurbinovo   Nicaea   Tigris

SARDINIA   Naples   Bari   Kastoria   Meteora   Salonika   Kayseri

Tyrrhenian Sea   Rossano   Arta   Nazianzus   Edessa

Palermo   Phocis   Chios   Binbir Kilise   Qal'at-Saman   Euphrates

Monreale   Cefalù   Daphni   Ephesus   Alahan Manastiri   R'safah

Carthage   Ionian Sea   Mistra   Athens   Tralles   Qalb Louzeh   Dura-Europos

SICILY   Palmyra

CRETE   CYPRUS

Bosra

Mediterranean Sea   Izra

Jerusalem

Bethlehem

Alexandria

Cairo

Sinai

0   300 miles   Bawit   Nile

Sohag

256

Bibliography

LATE CLASSICAL AND EARLY CHRISTIAN

BERCHEM, M. VAN, and CLOUZOT, E., *Mosaïques chrétiennes du IVᵉ au Xᵉ siècle*, Geneva, 1924

BEYER, H. W., *Der syrische Kirchenbau (Studien zur spätantiken Kunstgeschichte*, 1), Berlin, 1925

CABROL, F., et al., *Dictionnaire d'archéologie chrétienne et de liturgie*, Paris, 1908–53, 15 vols.

CECHELLI, C., *Il trionfo della croce*, Rome, 1953

DEICHMANN, F. W., *Frühchristliche Bauten und Mosaiken von Ravenna*, Baden-Baden, 1958

DELBRÜCK, R., *Die Konsulardiptychen und verwandte Denkmäler (Studien zur spätantiken Kunstgeschichte*, 2), Berlin, 1929

GERKE, F., *Die christlichen Sarkophage der vorkonstantinischen Zeit (Studien zur spätantiken Kunstgeschichte*, 11), Berlin, 1940

GERKE, F., *Spätantike und frühes Christentum*, Baden-Baden, 1967

GRABAR, A., *The Beginnings of Christian Art: 200–395*, London, 1967

GRABAR, A., *Martyrium*, Paris, 1943–46

KLAUSER, T., ed., *Reallexikon für Antike und Christentum*, Vol. I et seqq., Stuttgart, 1950–

KRAUTHEIMER, R., *Corpus Basilicarum Christianorum Romae*, Vatican City, 1939–

KRAUTHEIMER, R., *Early Christian and Byzantine Architecture*, Baltimore, 1965

MEER, F. VAN DER, *Altchristliche Kunst*, Cologne, 1960

MOREY, C. R., *Christian Art*, New York, 1935

MOREY, C. R., *Early Christian Art*, 2nd ed., Princeton, N. J., 1953

SIMSON, O. VON, *Sacred Fortress*, Chicago, 1948

TALBOT RICE, D., *The Beginnings of Christian Art*, London, 1957

VOLBACH, W. F., *Early Christian Art*, New York, 1961

VOLBACH, W. F., *Elfenbeinarbeiten der Spätantike und des frühen Mittelalters*, Mainz, 1952

WILPERT, J., *Die Malereien der Katakomben Roms*, Freiburg, 1903

WILPERT, J., *Die römischen Mosaiken und Malereien...*, Vols. I–IV, Freiburg, 1916

WIRTH, F., *Römische Wandmalerei vom Untergang Pompejis bis zum Ende des 3.Jahrhunderts*, Berlin, 1940

WULFF, O., *Altchristliche und byzantinische Kunst (Handbuch der Kunstwissenschaft*, Pts. I and II), Berlin, 1914–18

BYZANTIUM

HISTORY AND CIVILIZATION

BRÉHIER, L., *Le Monde byzantin*, Paris, 1948–50, 3 vols.

BURY, J. B., *A History of the Eastern Roman Empire from the Fall of Irene to the Accession of Basil I (802–867)*, London, 1912

BURY, J. B., *A History of the Later Roman Empire from Arcadius to Irene (395–800)*, London, 1889

BURY, J. B., *A History of the Later Roman Empire from the Death of Theodosius I to the Death of Justinian (395–565)*, London, 1923

GOUBERT, P., *Byzance avant l'Islam*, Vols. I and II, 1 and 2, Paris, 1956–65

HAUSSIG, H. W., *Kulturgeschichte von Byzanz*, 2nd ed., Stuttgart, 1966

HUNGER, H., *Reich der neuen Mitte: Der christliche Geist der byzantinischen Kultur*, Graz-Vienna-Cologne, 1965

OSTROGORSKY, G., *History of the Byzantine State*, Oxford, 1956

TALBOT RICE, D., *The Byzantines*, New York, 1962

TREITINGER, O., *Die oströmische Kaiser- und Reichsidee nach ihrer Gestaltung im höfischen Zeremoniell*, Jena, 1938; Darmstadt, 1956

ART: GENERAL SURVEYS

BECKWITH, J., *The Art of Constantinople. An Introduction to Byzantine Art: 330–1453*, London, 1961

DALTON, O. M., *Byzantine Art and Archaeology*, Oxford, 1911

DALTON, O. M., *East Christian Art: A Survey of the Monuments*, Oxford, 1925

DELVOYE, C., *L'Art byzantin*, Paris, 1967

DIEHL, C., *Byzantium: Greatness and Decline*, New Brunswick, N. J., 1957

DIEHL, C., *Manuel d'art byzantin*, 2nd ed., Paris, 1925–26, 2 vols.

DÖLGER, F., and SCHNEIDER, A. M., *Byzanz (Wissenschaftliche Forschungsberichte, Geisteswissenschaft*, 5th series), Bern, 1952

GRABAR, A., *Byzantium: Byzantine Art in the Middle Ages*, London, 1966

GRABAR, A., *The Golden Age of Justinian: From the Death of Theodosius to the Rise of Islam*, New York, 1967

PEIRCE, H., and TYLER, R., *L'Art byzantin*, Paris, 1932–34, 2 vols.

SAS-ZALOZIECKI, W., *Die altchristliche Kunst. Die byzantinische Kunst (Illustrierte Welt-Kunstgeschichte*, Vol. 2), Zurich, 1959

SCHWEINFURTH, P., *Die byzantinische Form: Ihr Wesen und ihre Wirkung*, 2nd ed., Berlin, 1962

STERN, H., *L'Art byzantin*, Paris, 1966

TALBOT RICE, D., *Art of the Byzantine Era*, New York, 1963

TALBOT RICE, D., *The Art of Byzantium*, New York, 1959

TALBOT RICE, D., *Byzantine Art*, London, 1954

VOLBACH, W. F., *Byzanz und der christliche Osten (Propyläen-Kunstgeschichte)*, Berlin, 1968

VOLBACH, W. F., et al., *L'Art byzantin*, Paris, 1933

WULFF, O., *Die byzantinische Kunst von der ersten Blüte bis zu ihrem Ausgang (Handbuch der Kunstwissenschaften)*, Berlin, 1914–18

ARCHITECTURE

BETTINI, S., *Il espacio arquitectonico de Roma a Bisancio*, Buenos Aires, 1963

CHOISY, A., *L'Art de bâtir chez les Byzantins*, Paris, 1883

DEICHMANN, F. W., *Studien zur Architektur Konstantinopels im 5. und 6. Jahrhundert nach Christus (Deutsche Beiträge zur Altertumswissenschaft, 4)*, Baden-Baden, 1956

EBERSOLT, J., *Le Grand Palais de Constantinople et le livre des cérémonies*, Paris, 1910

EBERSOLT, J., *Monuments d'architecture byzantine*, Paris, 1934

FORSYTH, G., and WEITZMANN, K., *The Church and Fortress of Justinian*, Ann Arbor, 1968

JANIN, R., *Constantinople byzantin: Développement urbain et répertoire topographique (Archives de l'Orient chrétien, 4)*, Paris, 1950 and 1964

KHATCHATRIAN, A., *Les Baptistères paléochrétiens*, Paris, 1962

MAMBOURY, E., and WIEGAND, T., *Die Kaiserpaläste von Konstantinopel zwischen Hippodrom und Marmarameer*, Berlin, 1934

MAVRODINOV, M., *Die byzantinische Architektur*, Sofia, 1955

SAS-ZALOZIECKI, W., *Geschichte der osteuropäischen christlichen Baukunst und ihre Abhängigkeit von Ost- und Westrom*, Berlin, 1930

SMITH, B., *Architectural Symbolism of Imperial Rome and the Middle Ages*, Princeton, N. J., 1956

SCULPTURE

BETTINI, S., *La scultura bizantina*, Florence, 1944 and 1946, 2 vols.

BRÉHIER, L., *La Sculpture et les arts mineurs byzantins (C. Diehl, Histoire de l'art byzantin, Vol. 3)*, Paris, 1936

DELVOYE, C., *La Sculpture byzantine jusqu'à l'époque iconoclaste (Corsi Ravennati, 8, pp. 177ff.)*, 1961

GRABAR, A., *La Décoration byzantine: Architecture et arts décoratifs*, Paris, 1928

GRABAR, A., *Sculptures byzantines de Constantinople: IVᵉ–Xᵉ siècle (Bibl. archéol. et hist. de l'Institut Français d'Archéologie d'Istanbul, 17)*, Paris, 1963

INAN, J., and ROSENBAUM, E., *Roman and Early Byzantine Portrait Sculpture in Asia Minor*, Oxford, 1966

KAUTSCH, R., *Kapitellstudien: Beiträge zu einer Geschichte des spätantiken Kapitells im Osten vom 4. bis ins 7. Jahrhundert (Studien zur spätantiken Kunstgeschichte, 9)*, Berlin, 1936

KOLLWITZ, J., *Oströmische Plastik der theodosianischen Zeit (Studien zur spätantiken Kunstgeschichte, 12)*, Berlin, 1941

LANGE, R., *Die byzantinische Reliefikone (Beiträge zur Kunst des christlichen Ostens, 1)*, Recklinghausen, 1964

WESSEL, K., *Byzantinische Plastik der palaiologischen Periode (Byzantion, 36, pp. 217ff.)*, 1966

PAINTING AND MOSAICS

AMMAN, A. M., *La pittura sacra bizantina*, Rome, 1957

BETTINI, S., *Frühchristliche Mosaiken*, Berlin, 1941

BETTINI, S., *La pittura bizantina*, Florence, 1938–39, 2 vols.

BOVINI, S., *Ravenna: I suoi mosaici e i suoi monumenti*, Florence, 1956

DEMUS, O., *Byzantine Mosaic Decoration: Aspects of Monumental Art in Byzantium*, Boston, 1950

DUFRENNE, S., *L'Illustration des psautiers grecs du moyen âge (Bibliothèque des cahiers archéol., I)*, Paris, 1966

EBERSOLT, J., *La Miniature byzantine*, Paris, 1926

FELICETTI-LIEBENFELS, W., *Geschichte der byzantinischen Ikonenmalerei von ihren Anfängen bis zum Ausklange unter Berücksichtigung der maniera greca und der italo-byzantinischen Schule*, Olten, 1956

GALASSI, G., *Roma o Bisanzio*, I: *I mosaici di Ravenna e le origini dell'arte italiana*; II: *Il congedo classico e l'arte nell'alto medioevo*, Rome, 1952–53

KITZINGER, E., *I mosaici di Monreale*, Palermo, 1960

LAZAREV, V, N., *Storia della pittura bizantina*, Turin, 1967

MATTHIAE, G., *Pittura romana del medioevo*, Vol. I, Rome, 1966

ONASCH, K., *Ikonen*, Berlin, 1961

PÄCHT, O., *Byzantine Illumination*, Oxford, 1952

RESTLE, M., *Die byzantinische Wandmalerei in Kleinasien*, Recklinghausen, 1967

WEITZMANN, K., *Illustrations in Roll and Codex: A Study on the Origin and Method of Text Illustration*, Princeton, N. J., 1947

MINOR ARTS

CECCHELLI, C., *La cattedra di Massimiano ed altri avorii romano-orientali*, Rome, 1936–44

DELBRÜCK, R., *Die Konsulardiptychen und verwandte Denkmäler (Studien zur spätantiken Kunstgeschichte, 2)*, Berlin, 1929

DODD, E. C., *Byzantine Silver Stamps*, with excursus: J. P. C. Kent, *The Comes Sacrarum Largitionum (Dumbarton Oaks Studies, 7)*, Washington, D. C., 1961

EBERSOLT, J., *Les Arts somptuaires de Byzance: Etude sur l'art Impérial de Constantinople*, Paris, 1924

GOLDSCHMIDT, A., and WEITZMANN, K., *Die byzantinischen Elfenbeinskulpturen des 10. bis 13. Jahrhunderts*, Berlin, 1930–34, 2 vols.

GRABAR, A., *Les Ampoules de Terre-Sainte: Monza-Bobbio*, Paris, 1958

KONDAKOV, N. P., *Les Costumes orientaux à la cour byzantine (Byzantion, I, pp. 7ff.)*, 1924

KONDAKOV, N. P., *Histoire et monuments des émaux byzantines*, Frankfurt, 1892

MATZULEWITSCH, L., *Byzantinische Antike: Studien auf Grund der Silbergefässe der Eremitage (Archäol. Mitt. aus russ. Sammlungen, 2)*, Berlin, 1929

MILLET, G., *Broderies religieuses de style byzantin (Bibliothèque de l'Ecole des Hautes Etudes, Sciences religieuses, 55)*, Paris, 1947

PASINI, A., *Il tesoro di San Marco in Venezia*, Venice, 1886

VOLBACH, W. F., *Das christliche Kunstgewerbe der Spätantike und des frühen Mittelalters im Mittelmeergebiet* (H. T. Bossert, *Geschichte des Kunstgewerbes aller Zeiten und Völker*, Vol. 5), Berlin, 1932

VOLBACH, W. F., *Elfenbeinarbeiten der Spätantike und des frühen Mittelalters* (*Römisch-Germanisches Zentralmuseum Mainz*, Catalogue 7), 2nd ed., Mainz, 1952

VOLBACH, W. F., *Metallarbeiten des christlichen Kultes in der Spätantike und im frühen Mittelalter* (*Römisch-Germanisches Zentralmuseum Mainz*, Catalogue 9), Mainz, 1921

WEITZMANN, K., *Die Elfenbeinkästen aus der mittelbyzantinischen Zeit*, Leipzig, 1930

WEITZMANN, K., et al., *A Treasury of Icons: Sixth to Seventeenth Centuries*, New York, 1967

WESSEL, K., *Die byzantinische Emailkunst vom 5. bis 13. Jahrhundert* (*Beiträge zur Kunst des christlichen Ostens*, 4), Recklinghausen, 1967

GREECE AND THE BALKAN COUNTRIES

BICEV, M., *Die Architektur in Bulgarien: Von der ältesten Zeit bis zur Befreiung 1788*, Sofia, 1961

BIHALJI-MERIN, O., *Byzantine Frescoes and Icons in Yugoslavia*, New York, 1960

BOSCHKOW, A., *Bulgarian Art*, Sofia, 1964

BOSKOVIC, D., *L'Art médiéval en Serbie et Macédoine*, Belgrade, 1949

CRANAKI, M., and EDELSTEIN, S., *Grèce byzantine*, Lausanne, 1962

DIEHL, C., et al., *Les Monuments chrétiens de Salonique*, Paris, 1918, 2 vols.

DYGGVE, E., *History of Salonikan Christianity*, Oslo, 1951

FILOV, B. D., *Geschichte der altbulgarischen Kunst bis zur Eroberung des bulgarischen Reiches durch die Türken*, Berlin-Leipzig, 1932

GRABAR, A., *La Peinture religieuse en Bulgarie* (*Orient et Byzance*, 1), Paris, 1928

GRABAR, A., and OPRESCU, G., *Rumänien: Bemalte Kirchen in der Moldau*, Munich, 1962

HAMANN-MACLEAN, R., and HALLENSLEBEN, H., *Die Monumentalmalerei in Serbien und Makedonien vom 11. bis zum frühen 14. Jahrhundert* (*Osteuropastudien des Landes Hessen*, 2nd series, 3–5), Giessen, 1963

HODDINOT, R. F., *Early Byzantine Churches in Macedonia and Southern Serbia: A Study of the Origins and the Initial Development of East Christian Art*, London, 1963

LEMERLE, P., *Philippes et la Macédoine orientale à l'époque chrétienne et byzantine*, Paris, 1945

MAVRODINOV, N., *Die altbulgarische Malerei* (in Bulgarian, with German résumé), Sofia, 1946

Medieval Bulgarian Culture, Sofia, 1964

MILLET, G., *L'Ecole grècque dans l'architecture byzantine* (*Bibliothèque de l'Ecole des Hautes Etudes, Sciences religieuses*, 26), Paris, 1916

MYLONAS, P. M., *Athos: Forms in a Sacred Space*, Athens, 1965

PROTIC, A., *L'Architecture religieuse bulgare*, Sofia, 1924

SOTIRIOU, G., *Christian and Byzantine Archaeology* (in Greek), Athens, 1942

SOTIRIOU, G., *The Early Christian Churches of Greece* (in Greek), Athens, 1931

STEFANESCU, I. D., *Contribution à l'étude des peintures murales valaques* (*Orient et Byzance*, 3), Paris, 1928

STYLIANOU, A., and STYLIANOU, J., *The Painted Churches in Cyprus*, Stourbridge, 1964

TALBOT RICE, D., *The Icons of Cyprus*, London, 1937

TALBOT RICE, D., and RADOJCIC, S., *Jugoslawien: Mittelalterliche Fresken*, Munich, 1955

WULFF, O., *Das Katholikon von Hosios Lukas und verwandte Kirchenbauten*, Berlin, n. d.

RUSSIA

AINALOV, D. W., *Geschichte der russischen Monumentalkunst der vormoskowitischen Zeit*, Berlin-Leipzig, 1923

AINALOV, D. W., *Geschichte der russischen Monumentalkunst zur Zeit des Grossfürstentums Moskau*, Berlin, 1933

ALPATOV, M. W., *Altrussische Ikonenmalerei*, Dresden, 1958

ALPATOV, M. W., *Art Treasures of Russia*, New York, 1967

AMIRANASHVILI, S., *Medieval Georgian Enamels of Russia*, New York, 1964

L'Art byzantin chez les Slaves: Recueil dédié à la mémoire de Th. Uspenskij, Vol. 2: *L'Ancienne Russie*, Paris, 1932

BALTRUSAITIS, J., *Etudes sur l'art médiéval en Géorgie et en Arménie*, Paris, 1929

BLANKOFF, J., *L'Art de la Russie ancienne*, Brussels, 1963

CHUBINASHVILI, G. N., *Georgian Goldsmith's Work of the Eighth to Eighteenth Centuries* (in Russian, with German translation), Tiflis, 1957

DER NERSESSIAN, S., *Armenia and the Byzantine Empire*, Cambridge, Mass., 1945

DOURNOVO, L. A., *Armenian Miniatures*, New York, 1961

GRABAR, I. E., et al., ed., *History of Russian Art* (in Russian), Vol. I, Moscow, 1953; German ed.: *Geschichte der russischen Kunst*, Vol. I, Dresden, 1957

IPSIROGLU, M. S., *Die Kirche von Achthamar: Bauplastik im Leben des Lichts*, Berlin-Mainz, 1963

LANG, D. M., *The Georgians*, New York, 1966

LAZAREV, V. N., *Old Russian Murals and Mosaics from the Eleventh to the Sixteenth Century*, London, 1966

LEBEDEVA, J., *Andrej Rubljow und seine Zeitgenossen*, Dresden, 1962

LUKOMSKI, G. K., *L'Architecture russe du XIᵉ au XVIIᵉ siècle*, Paris, 1929

LUKOMSKI, G. K., *L'Art décoratif russe*, Paris, 1928

ONASCH, K., *Ikonen: Altrussische Kunstdenkmäler*, Berlin, 1961

RÉAU, L., *L'Art russe*, Paris, 1945

TALBOT RICE, T., *A Concise History of Russian Art*, New York, 1963

TALBOT RICE, T., *Russian Art*, London, 1949

TIKHOMIROV, M. N., *The Towns of Ancient Rus*, Moscow, 1959

VERNADSKIJ, G., *Kievan Russia*, New Haven, 1948

VOYCE, A., *The Moscow Kremlin: Its History, Architecture, and Art Treasures*, Berkeley, 1954

WEITZMANN, K., *Die armenische Buchmalerei des 10. und beginnenden 11. Jahrhunderts*, Bamberg, 1933

Index

Photo credits: Alinari, Florence, p. 21, 26, 38, 44, 48, 53, 78, 80–82, 83 upper, 92, 191. Anderson, Florence, p. 35, 36, 95, 126, 127. Lala Aufsberg, Sonthofen, p. 155, 187, 188. Kunstgewerbemuseum, Berlin-Dahlem, p. 183. Münzkabinett, State Museums, Berlin (East), p. 31. E. Böhm, Mainz, p. 37, 107, 108, 110–12, 113 upper, 114–16, 154, 159, 164, 177, 192–204. O. Böhm, Venice, p. 174 lower, 179. Boudot-Lamotte, Paris, p. 25, 223, 239. Magyar Nemreti Museum, Budapest, p. 182. Bulloz, Paris, p. 27, 52, 163. M. Carrieri, Milan, p. 129. N. Cirani, Milan, p. 243. De Antonis, Rome, p. 22, 33, 79, 83 lower. Cathedral Treasury, Esztergom, p. 176. J. Freeman, London, p. 185. A. Held, Écublens, p. 14–16, 18, 19, 74, 145, 146, 218. Hirmer Fotoarchiv, Munich, p. 20, 23, 39, 45–47, 50, 55 (2×), 56, 67 (2×), 75, 86, 91, 98, 101, 102, 119, 124, 132, 133 (2×), 148, 185. Holle Verlag, Baden-Baden, p. 13, 17, 28, 32, 41, 43, 54, 59, 62, 64, 68, 71, 73 upper, 77, 85, 87, 88, 90, 93, 96, 100, 103, 105, 106, 121, 122, 130, 136, 138, 144, 147, 151–53, 168, 169, 186, 206–11, 214, 215, 217, 221, 224–27, 229–31, 240, 241, 246, 247, 252. M. Kontos, Athens, p. 118, 150 upper, 156–58, 160–62, 205. J.-A. Lavaud, Paris, p. 60, 184. G. Likides, Salonika, p. 150 lower. British Museum, London, p. 57, 69, 70, 123. Victoria & Albert Museum, London, p. 66. Luisa, Brescia, p. 58, 61, 63, 120, 134 lower. Mazzari, Milan, p. 89, 99. Torp, Oslo, p. 149. Archives Photographiques, Paris, p. 84. Bibliothèque Nationale, Paris, p. 29, 30 (2×), 73 lower, 142, 143, 166, 170, 173. Marcella Pedone, Milan, p. 141. A. Perissinotto, Padua, p. 109, 113 lower, 212, 213, 216, 220, 222. La Photothèque Européenne, Paris, p. 128. J. Powell, Rome, p. 117. M. Pucciarelli, Rome, p. 34, 49. J. Remmer, Munich, p. 174 upper, 175, 178, 180, 181, 189, 190, 228, 232–38, 242, 244, 245, 248–51. Biblioteca Apostolica Vaticana, Rome, p. 72, 167, 171, 172. Museo Torlonia, Rome, p. 24. Scala, Florence, p. 40, 42, 51, 76, 104, 135. Schmölz & Ullrich, Cologne, p. 65. M. Seidel, Mittenwald, p. 134 upper. Steinkopf, Berlin, p. 165. Cathedral Treasury, Trier, p. 125. Österreichische Nationalbibliothek, Vienna, p. 137, 139, 140. Villari e Figli, Bologna, p. 94, 97. Dumbarton Oaks Collection, Washington, D.C., p. 131.

The map was drawn from the author's sketch by J. J. G. M. Delfgaauw, Baden-Baden.